'What a b⋯⋯⋯⋯⋯⋯⋯⋯⋯⋯ – I'm
trying to ⋯⋯⋯⋯⋯⋯⋯⋯⋯ ⋯one of
them do it justice'

'I ⋯⋯⋯⋯ read such a succinct and unsparing chronicle of
the destruction of body and spirit that can be brought about
by the violation of a child. It's the equivalent of a letter from a
gulag, except that the events take place in Sussex in the 1980s…
The saving grace is the writer's pleasure in scholarship, and his
undaunted eye for the beauty of the world'

Hilary Mantel

'A beautifully written account – both brilliant and appalling – of
the psychological consequences of sexual abuse of the author
when he was a vulnerable boy by a priest… Rarely have I felt
so angry'

Henry Marsh

'Sometimes all we can do in the face of evil is name it; and the
naming is the only victory we get over it. But it takes courage,
immense courage, to be the one who calls out the name. That is
what makes this book an act of pure heroism'

Richard Holloway

'*Paper Cuts* is harrowing, but never gratuitously so, and in
between the vivid and looping confrontations with past trauma,
we follow Bernard's joyous, precarious and often intellectually
brilliant thought processes'

Julia Blackburn

'It is an extraordinary book in its unblinking truthfulness, even more so in its refusal to deny the complexities and ambiguity that follow such childhood trauma'

Observer

'Compelling... Bernard lays rightful claim to the role of the truth-teller ... to construct a historical document that will enclose the trauma and allow him to "get on with living my life"'

Times Literary Supplement

'The form in which Bernard presents his thoughts, his memories, his perceptions, is liturgical. Moments emerge, dissolve, shape themselves round each other... It's both a testament of great documentary usefulness and a really beautiful piece of art'

Guardian

STEPHEN BERNARD

Stephen Bernard is an internationally award-winning essayist, editor, and bibliographer at the University of Oxford. He occasionally writes for the *Times Literary Supplement*.

STEPHEN BERNARD

Paper Cuts

VINTAGE

1 3 5 7 9 10 8 6 4 2

Vintage
20 Vauxhall Bridge Road,
London SW1V 2SA

Vintage is part of the Penguin Random House group
of companies whose addresses can be found
at global.penguinrandomhouse.com

 Penguin
Random House
UK

First published in Vintage in 2019
First published in hardback by Jonathan Cape in 2018

penguin.co.uk/vintage

A CIP catalogue record for this book is available from
the British Library

ISBN 9781784707040

Printed and bound in Great Britain by Clays Ltd, Elcograf S.p.A.

Penguin Random House is committed to a sustainable future for our
business, our readers and our planet. This book is made from Forest
Stewardship Council® certified paper.

To Phoebe and Ric

Falkirk Community Trust	
30124 03124119 5	
Askews & Holts	
B BER	£8.99
GM	

A NOTE FROM THE AUTHOR

The names of the people in this book have been changed apart from those of myself, my family, my therapist Dr Richard Gipps, significant literary figures, and, most importantly, that of my abuser: Canon T.D. Fogarty. This is not done to confuse the reader, but to protect the identities of private individuals who have nonetheless done remarkable personal and public service, often at great cost to themselves. They should be lauded, but never sought such approbation, and it is not my intention or place now to put them in the spotlight.

It will become clear that I have been very lucky in my family, my few friends, and doctors. Not all are so fortunate. I commend those who struggle without such support.

I am not a writer, but an academic, with my own idiolect, for example giving patronymics when talking about people, including my family and friends. I have not sought to disguise these verbal tics and hope you will excuse me for them.

This book was largely written over a period of six weeks during a course of trauma therapy with Dr Richard Gipps. The statement printed in this book is a redacted version of the actual statement I made to Sussex Police.

My benchmark in writing this book was to be as honest as I could; I wrote it for myself, but share it with you now. Without honesty, we are nothing in the world, or not much. I hope that comes across. To be accountable for oneself and one's conduct are, to me, the most important tests one can set oneself in life.

Stephen Bernard

STEPHEN BERNARD AT THE AGE OF TWELVE

From: Stephen Bernard

To: Dr Richard Gipps

Date: 31 December 2015 at 00:45

Subject: narrative about my childhood

Dear Dr Gipps,

I hope you are very well.

I had a lovely Christmas.

I have been thinking hard about what we need
to do and have started a narrative which it may
be helpful for you to see. I do not want or expect you to become my writing master and so
have only included the first page. I think that
you can see there is a certain calmness and detachment to it, and that it also hints at what
is to come and some of the ambivalences that
may come with it.

See you next week.

Stephen

PAPER CUTS

PAPER CUTS.

There will be some merit in getting my thoughts down on paper, after all this, that. It has taken some time to get this far, and some trouble too. Has it been worth taking the trouble, I wonder? Will it be worth the trouble to do this? I am just one; there have been many. The stories of each of them, of us, must be worth the telling (I think).

I will start with my own story, of a day in January 2016, and of the trouble I went to to write an essay about a man who lived some time ago, who left his mark on the world by shepherding the present into the future. There were others, of course, but I choose him, choose one, to illustrate my point. He is the most important to me, then, now.

Today I construct the self. Each day I construct the self. From the waste hours of sleep I wake and, stiff of limb and muddled in mind, I wonder who I am and where I am. In the darkness I reach for the iPad, my iPad (I don't think). What is the time? I know that there is such a thing as time, although I am at that moment out of it. Five o'clock, just gone.

I urinate in the bathroom. I remember somehow – on the sudden – upstairs somewhere and another time. And the shame. Well. I brush my teeth. It has gone five (I think).

I go to the desk in my study and open the blinds. It is still dark out. I look at the computer. I switch it on. Click. I look at *The Times* online. Click. Bowie's dead. No! Surely this means something. Surely I know what I'm doing, more than I'm letting on.

What a lucky planet we were to have had David Bowie. So lucky. Imagine how vast all of space and time is – how endless and empty, how black and cold. Imagine a tracking shot across the universe, nothing happening nearly everywhere, nearly all the time.

And then, as it scrolls past our galaxy, you can hear, quiet at first, but getting louder as we close in, Rebel Rebel, coming from our planet, from

our country, in our time, playing on tinny tran-
sistor radios, in a million bedrooms, as a whole
generation, and the next, and the next, straight-
en their spines, and feel their pulses rise, and say:
'This. This is how I feel. Or at least, this is how I
feel now. Now I've heard this.'

I switch the kettle on in the kitchen and brew some coffee. This will wake me up, make me present and correct
in the world. I switch the radio on. There's been an accident, somewhere I've never heard of. Uninterested, I
take my coffee to the desk.

On my desk there's a silver frame with the picture of a
young woman in it. She is in a wedding dress, her wedding
dress (I think). She looks happy. Coffee. Sip. Who is that
man? Who is that man next to her? Him. In the dove-grey,
white-shirted suit. He must be her husband, or her hus-
band-to-be. On the threshold: my father. I do not remember the face, but I must have had a father (I think). Father.

I switch on the television on the wall in my study. 'Ziggy
Stardust' plays. Now there is both the sound of the radio
from the kitchen and that of the TV curdling-electric in
my flat. Outside no bird sings. I am in Jericho and far

from the Meadows. Inside it's warm, but outside there's a chill as cold as no wonder.

I wash and go to my room – light; light but none outside – and get dressed. Clean clothes – look sharp! – look smart to face the day.

Medication. And a cigarette outside the pub over the road. There is a chill, after all. Hello, the house!

*

I feel in my pocket as I smoke. Here is a letter to someone.

> Today you construct the self. Each day you construct the self ...

It is a letter from me, to me.

> You become the self as the day develops.

> You are stiff because of the medication. You went to bed at eight, but were not asleep at midnight.

> Have you taken your medication?

A letter from the night-time to face the day. I stub out my cigarette and re-enter my flat opposite. Someone's got the radio and the TV on. Have you taken your medication?

One tablet. Two tablets. Four tablets. Nine tablets. Today will be the day. Today will be the day when it all gets right. You can put it right. Swallow. The self. In a bottle.

*

You swallow the ketamine, which you have been prescribed for your condition, with the orange squash. Time passes.

*

Welcome. To. The. Multiverse! An infinity of meaning in an ununaspirated letter. Suddenly, on a sudden, and in a moment – now! A year passes – or was that just a minute? The child of the past breaks out from the infinity of meaning and now – before you know it – all time is there, is here, is now. This sentence is about nothing but itself. But already it is about other sentences, framing its meaning, and the multiverse reigns, as a bull in a china shop. Infinitudes like a, like a fugue in the mind.

*

I read the *Whitehall Evening Post* for 14 January 1705. Every day now for five years I have read the day's newspapers of the day since 1 January 1701. It is my secret, which I tell you now. I read the news of the day, and then read some of the books published that day. I know what happens next, but I kid myself I do not. I totally immerse myself in the eighteenth century. Before I die, I know, Alexander Pope's *Dunciads* will be published and I will probably die with Henry Fielding's *Tom Jones* in my hand. The rise of the novel, as scholars used to call it. Except, so far, there's not much of a novel to speak of. Nor is there any *Spectator* coming daily from the press and being republished in volume form yearly for the rest of the eighteenth century. Today Thomas Betterton the actor is ill. Next week, I know he will deliver one of the greatest performances of his career – of the eighteenth century – but for the moment he has a cholic and is not expected to last.

I go to conferences, academic conferences, and people say things like 'Godolphin was at a nervous point in his career ...' Too right! I think – he had a lot to be nervous about. Right now it's all about the duke of Marlborough. And the funny thing is that there are almost no women. Where are all the women (I think)?

In the archive. Hardly in the press, or coming from the press. Sometimes someone will appear in history, in time, who stands beyond the archive, whose story will last. Men – and women – so remarkable, or whose work is so sublime – or horrific – that they cannot be contained in the archive. Marlborough was such a man. There have been others.

★

I wake now with a voice which is clean and sharp and precise, unlike anything else I have written. I write without reference to the past, in the present of the past. Godolphin! You shape-shifter.

I went to bed at eight but was not asleep at midnight and so had to take the same dose of antipsychotics and sedatives again. I have just woken up. Last night I wrote a thousand words for waking up today, to send to myself, a thousand-word letter she told me to write to myself, so I could understand myself when I woke up (because I'm sedated, I have forgotten who I am). What a brilliant idea! I am – the self-constructed self – am the brilliant idea taken from the mind of her and written out to tell you who you are and what to do and what you do. This.

You are Stephen Bernard, of the University of Oxford.

I am Stephen Bernard, of the University of Oxford.

★

The life of the mind. The mind in dialogue with itself.

★

one dark night. one dark. one dark night. fired with love's urgent longings. urgent longings.

in darkness and concealment

★

It is eight thirty. I need to go to the Bodleian Library. I go down Walton Street on my bike (I cycle only in my mind, in my rapidly cycling mind). Down St Giles. Across, past the Martyrs' Memorial. Wait! I look around me.

★

O. O. mag. num. mys. ter. ium. It comes again, that 'complication', that simple complicated thought: para- noia, which at first I do not see as such. The thought that someone, somewhere, has malevolent intent. That thought. That nebulous insistent thought. Paranoia. That Wreck of the Hesperus: there is the sheer fact of it, distorted, undistorted and distorting. Afterwards the body of the captain's daughter – the hurt and confused sureness of it – lies on the shore of the mind, a memory of the certainty of the captain. Dead, but a fact that will condition my experience of life – my life – ever after.

*

First I seek some quiet, some stillness in the morning before the day before me. I turn into Beaumont Street and walk with purpose past the doctors' surgeries and the dentists' to Worcester College at the corner of Beaumont Street and Walton Street. I cross at the crossing.

I enter under the black iron gates and go through the porters' lodge. They notice me, but I go unnoticed, as I have so many mornings in these the years of my life.

Slowly, carefully, I descend the steps into the sunken garden of the college and go out through the gate of the quad into the gardens of the eighteenth century. I walk towards the waters. Such quiet! Such stillness. The air is crisp and expectant of the day that contains it, and I make my way round the lakes, past the bridge and to the cricket pavilion.

No one is around in the early morning and the greenness of the playing field is generous in its bright colour.

I light a cigarette. Five minutes pass, then ten.

I must get on. I have a full day ahead of me. But I am thankful for this, for the gardens of Worcester College.

*

I see a man walking towards me. In a light-brown tweed greatcoat. I would like that tweed greatcoat to replace mine. It is cold outside today, in these the mansions of my house. I slept in St Giles, North Gate. I don't know where I will sleep tonight, whether I'll have the change, the money for a bed. He comes closer and nods, then turns, gives me change, but not enough. He looks kind, but troubled. It is so cold. This place is cold, Christminster.

*

I walk with small strides along Broad Street and under the great gates of the sixteenth-century library. I cross over the threshold. I have a great deal to do today. I have to write that article for the *TLS*. I am at the security gate in the Proscholium. Card.

Now I climb the heavy black-brown Tudor stairs to Duke Humfrey's Library. My legs are also heavy. Forty is not a great age to have reached, but age is catching up with me. I catch my breath at the turn in the stair. I must stop smoking.

It is quiet, not very busy today in the Library. I find a desk, my desk. I look around and wonder who else is in the Library today. I wonder who else has sat here at this desk and written about the past, about literature. Edmond Malone for one, I know sat here, a great literary scholar, possibly writing the letters that are kept in the Library today. It's chilly in the January morning air outside, but inside somehow it's as warm. Right. I must write.

> *Bernard Lintot was, in conscious rivalry with his contemporaries the Tonsons, the preeminent bookseller of the early eighteenth century, towering over the rest . . .*

★

Sherborne School, with its deep yellow stones and pink, fire-damaged Abbey, lies in a wide, clear vale on the North Dorset Downs. It is an institution which was re-founded by King Edward VI, having its origins in the medieval monastery attached to the Abbey. It is styled on an Oxford college, with its large mullion-windowed quad; with the Abbey to the south and, to the north, an entrance tower; with its tower and sculpture of the young king's coat of arms over the gate. It is a public school of some renown, for five centuries turning out the sons of the gentry, leaders of the state and the state church.

It was here that I arrived as a fifteen-year-old boy, to start a new life. A son of the navy and of the Dock Road in Liverpool, I had by dint of academic merit won a scholarship to the school. The school and its masters were to transform me, a Scouser with a broad Scouse accent. It was to give me a new voice, the modulated soft vowels of received pronunciation, and ultimately to give me a voice which would speak the reasons why a fifteen-year-old boy would choose to leave his home and family and start again.

*

… when I consider how much I have seen, read and heard, I begin to blame my own

Taciturnity; and since I have neither Time nor Inclination to communicate the Fulness of my Heart in Speech, I am resolved to do it in Writing; and to Print my self out, if possible, before I Die. I have been often told by my Friends, that it is Pity so many useful Discoveries which I have made, should be in the Possession of a Silent Man.

Thus Joseph Addison, thus Stephen Bernard.

*

Is it possible to love cancer? Is it possible to be in love with cancer? Not the condition, but the cancer itself? When I was a child I had such a cancer and I think I loved it. This is not a story about cancer, but a story about love.

When I was a child, I spake as a child, I understood as a child, I thought as a child: but when I became a man, I put away childish things. But I still spoke as a child and that was how I learnt to speak my love.

Loving cancer is a disgrace. It is a shameful thing to do. Loving cancer means never having to say you are sorry.

*

When did Praxiteles see me naked? No, wait. When did Fogarty first see me naked? 8 September 1987. I was just a boy, not yet a man. The date is clear in my mind. It happened when I returned from my first day at my new school, in a new town, in a new country. Something had happened to my father and mother. I did not know what, I do not know what. I am honest, they are honest. The father is honest, the mother is honest, the son is honest. But that does not mean that they know everything. There is a prize in not knowing. Some things are so toxic that they cannot be known, can only be felt. I felt that something had happened to my mother and father, but that it was toxic. Why else would they move from their homeland, and move to this, to what happened, to what happened to me?

Canon Thomas 'Dermod' Fogarty. A doctor of divinity, a doctor of canon law. A distinguished man with a distinguished air. He was, as the books would have it, tall, dark, and handsome. Simple, useful words. Clichéd, but true. He wore black clothes and black shoes, with a simple dog collar – and in winter a black cape, a remnant from his days at the English College in Rome. But it was September and he was not in Rome or thinking of being in Rome. He was in Sussex, his parish, and had come to bless the house.

Where was my mother? I did not know, do not know. He came to the door. The first day at a new school, in a new house, and I was eager. Priests were part of life. Canon Fogarty had come to bless the house, our new home. He came to the door while I was getting changed and boy! how this would change me. He explained that he was the parish priest and that he had come to bless the house. Those were welcome words, and kind and loving to a boy who had grown up in the love of the Church, in another country. They meant no harm. Maybe, I think now, he meant no harm. I was in my gym kit and answered the door. Here was a vision of black, in black, simple and kind and loving. He brought blessings to the house, my home, our home.

*

Post hoc, ergo propter hoc. Latin, the language of the ancients, the language of Catullus, the language of love. The language of Martial – love, frustrated and bitter and wrong. Also, the language of the law. Fogarty taught me Latin and brought love and the law into my life. He meant to bring only love, but life is not that simple. Love is regulated. The language of love is regulated. Nominative, accusative. The name, Fogarty, the accusation? We shall see.

The law is a massive and unrelenting force to be brought into the life of a child. It is not the law that protects the child, but the man who protects the child. Where was my mother? I do not know. Where was my father? That is an easier answer.

Gerard Bernard was a naval man. He had been present at the conception of his children, but not much else, it seemed to me as a child. He had a country to defend, another country. Where was he when all this happened? Abroad. Perhaps that is why as a child I used to think that I hated abroad, and like Charles Wilcox thought I saw through foreigners so. Foreigners are those with whom we deal diplomatically, or militarily, when we have to. In short, my father was abroad.

Our last parish priest we had called father, but Fogarty was a canon. I called him 'Father' at first, but that was wrong he explained to me. He was 'Canon', a canon of the diocese and a doctor of canon law.

The canon law is not the law. Canon law is the body of law which regulates life for a Catholic. It exists in perfect international unity with the Church, within the Church. To know Latin, to speak Latin, is to speak a dead language, perfect in itself. The language of canon law is Latin; the language of canon law is a dead language, perfect in itself.

Canon law is not the law, but it is the law of the Church. Fogarty was a doctor of canon law, a law parallel to the law of the land. This was a new country to me and to my family. The law of this country was not the law of the land. The law of this country was canon law, perfect in itself.

Naval children, when they are in a new country, do not know the law. They do not know their country or the country in which they live. Naval children know the law of the navy, naval law. What happens when an irresistible force meets an immovable object? There is an impact, but nothing moves or changes. English, my language, the language of my country, my law, was about to meet Latin, the language of the law by which we were meant to live. *Post hoc, ergo propter hoc*. The language of Catullus and Martial, but also Newman. But it was not the language of love to me. Not uncomplicated, unsophisticated love. My love was a love for something bigger than that, which rightly thought it was bigger than that. My language was not English or Latin, but the language of cancer, a language which is both the irresistible force and the immovable object. Entire in itself. Perfect from the moment of conception.

*

I am a doctor of philosophy, but that does not mean that I understand philosophy. There are a lot of doctors in this story. Fogarty was a doctor of canon law. I am a professor of English; I profess English for my job. This story will set doctor against doctor, professor against professor. Fogarty was my confessor, he confessed for his job. This story will set confessor against confessor.

In English there are two ways of pronouncing the word confessor. One means the man who hears the confession: one means the man who confesses. Fogarty was not that man. He did not confess.

English has become my life. Another language, my own native language. English is the language of life to me, of my life. I spake only as a child is the expression of the perfect thought, expressed perfectly, in my language. The Bible is, to me, an English Bible. This story is the story of the conquest of the Latin world, the language of the two largest constituencies the world has ever known: the Roman Empire and the Roman Catholic Church; and the largest constituency the world will ever know: the British Empire, the Empire of English.

*

That thought again. That thought, that somewhere someone is plotting, against me. In darkness and concealment. O. O. Against me. I do not know why, cannot know why. It is a fact, that will tincture my thoughts, my thinking, my day, as it has so often. myster. ium.

*

Of all the statements I could make, it would be wrong to say none are true. No, none is true. None is singular. It was a moment of revelation when I realized that 'none is' was correct. None of these statements is true. That is the correct thing to say.

I have made statements, to the police, to the authorities. None is true, is true. That is a statement, but it is not true. This is true.

There is the feeling of a strong and heavy hand on my neck. I cannot move my head because of this. I can't breathe.

This is true.

I can see the Canon in the mirror. His trousers are round his ankles. He is above and behind me. I feel the boniness and weight of him in me. In me.

This is true.

I wake up. I'm at home. I feel the stickiness of the semen, which reminds me of Fogarty's semen on my back. I'm very scared. I can't breathe.

This is true.

I gently remove the hand – Fogarty's – from my thigh it comes back it moves towards my groin I do not want this to happen again I can't breathe I'm only little this is wrong I'm scared I can't breathe I'm all by myself with this man he tells me to go upstairs I have no choice I am electric

This is true.

My back is awkward I move and this causes a sudden penetrating force the weight is inside me and intense and above me behind my back green and beige a mirror with an open door in it

I am electric

*

I should perhaps tell you how embedded I would become in the Church – almost to the point of being in a cult. Each morning on weekdays at seven I would serve mass with the Canon in the convent chapel. Then I would go to the grammar school; then I would attend the Canon in the presbytery and all that that entailed. On Saturdays, I would serve mass with him in the chapel at the King Edward VII Hospital on the Downs. On Sundays, I would serve mass with the Canon at eight and ten thirty in the morning and then at benediction or vespers, depending on the point in the liturgical calendar, at six. My mother was on the parish council; my sister attended the convent school; my father was abroad. Each day, after my prayers for release, I would sleep and then be rereleased into a world without forgiveness, with forgiveness. There was no fixed point outside the Church from which I could move the world, so I stayed within it, fixated by it.

*

This is not getting it done (I think). I idle the minutes away before my books. They want the copy at the *TLS* today. I must start again.

It is not surprising that Tonson has received the most critical attention of any bookseller of the period, but . . .

*

It is 8 September 1987. I am at home, in my new home. It is 14 January 2016. I am at home, in my new home. I am in Oxford and I am living in the eighteenth century. That is my time, my place.

Nothing happened in the eighteenth century, and nothing was perfectly expressed. Everything was perfectly expressed in the eighteenth century, in England, in English. And the Universal Enemy was the Catholic Church.

I study manuscripts, letters. My job is not to express things, but to copy things. To copy them out, and in doing so to transcend the time in which they were written and to make them something outside of time.

I don't have a voice, only a subject. The subject is the creation of literature, and the conditions which brought it about, the creation of the English literary canon.

I am electric

*

I have read a few books. I have read many books, but I only remember a few. *Clarissa. The Curious Incident of the Dog in the Night-time. Disgrace. Finnegans Wake. Some Hope.* I don't know much about art, but I know what I like. I like Richardson, Haddon, Coetzee, Joyce, St Aubyn. Nothing else. I don't really rate literature or art. It doesn't speak to me. It isn't my job to explain it. I can't understand or explain the art of these men. How did it come about, though? That I can explain, that I can understand.

I have met the author of *Disgrace*. I know the author of the *Curious Incident*, although he does not know about these paper cuts. Joyce, obviously, I haven't met, although I think I know him best. I know the author of my experiences, my self: Fogarty.

Something happened to me when I was a child that was to be my experience. Do I know authors? Yes. Do I like authors? Yes. Do I trust authors? No. There is something about the artificiality of what they create which I cannot trust. I cannot trust their artifice. I cannot trust their art. I trust what is true, and what is true is that authors are not to be trusted.

There are three consummate artists whom one has to have something to say about in the eighteenth century: Dryden, Swift, Pope. The Augustans. Dryden expressed things perfectly, transforming the language of the ancients into a language we can understand today. Pope expressed things perfectly too, transforming the language we can understand today into a language for eternity. Swift expressed what he saw, and what he saw was not right. Swift's is an imperfect language, expressing imperfection. Who survives, who will survive of these three? Swift. These three at the beginning of the eighteenth century speak for themselves, but Swift speaks to today.

I have measured myself against these three men. I think I owe them that, and that I owe that to myself. Dryden speaks to today in what he did not write. He lived in a country in fear of the Universal Enemy. Terrorists! They were everywhere. Titus Oates was a priest, a man of the cloth, but was he to be trusted? He told the country what it wanted to hear, that the Roman Catholic Church was plotting the overthrow of the Kingdom, of the order of creation. The Church was plotting the overthrow of the natural, the right order of things.

Dryden was a Catholic in a time and a country when to be Catholic was to be suspect. He did not talk in his letters about his religion, only about those of 'our perwasion'. What persuasion was that? It was a persuasion which dare not speak its name. Dryden speaks to us today in what he did not say, in his silences. His sons were true sons of the Church. He did not discuss them. They had gone to Rome to study, they had gone to Raqqa.

Pope, too, was Catholic. The greatest of the Augustans, he spoke for himself and not in silences. He mocked authority, but he was authority. The author of his own creation, he created the shade of those laurels which descended to him. His closest friend, Swift, was told that he would not be a poet by his cousin Dryden. These three men were poets, but only one was something else, an author: Swift. To Swift we will return, as he returns to us, speaking our language, not that of the ancients or of eternity.

*

Sussex at the end of the twentieth century was a fine place, well placed. It was the place of my adolescence. I came to Sussex as a child from another country and left a man. There is something about the Sussex Downs in autumn that speaks to the soul. The lanes of Sussex, the fields, the rapture. God was in Sussex and saw that it was good.

I was a Catholic, in Catholic country. Sussex is the country of the Fitzalan-Howards, the dukes of Norfolk. The Church has found sanctuary in Sussex, under the protection of the family of the Earl Marshall, under the protection of its saints and martyrs. Midhurst, the town of my adolescence, the town at the heart of the Downs, has its own presiding martyr: Blessed Margaret Pole. She has a simple side chapel in the church there. She was ransomed in the castle there, now in ruins. Someone truly good held captive in the sixteenth century, held in Sussex against her wishes, bequeathing her faith to her captors. Her successors in that country bear witness to her faith, to truth.

There are very few voices in my story, which may seem strange, but it is not so strange as what those few voices say.

'My son, would you like to make your confession to me?'

'Forgive me, father, for I have sinned. It is some time since I made my last confession.'

*

St Mary's Presbytery sits in the heart of Midhurst, in the heart of the South Downs, of Sussex. A modern building, it replaced a mansion in the middle of the twentieth century. Yellowstone red brick, it was built by faith, and the money of the Irish. The old house, which I never saw, had tennis courts, and a wall that surrounded it. It had gardens and large grounds, now built over by the prospectors of the baby boom. The tennis courts are gone, but the wall remains, in parts, surrounding the new church which Nicolas Pevsner so admired. A statement of faith in the future of the Church and of the Church in Sussex, a statement of the faith of the Church today. The Norfolks were the presiding influence over the new church in Midhurst. There is a convent attached to it too, which had a private school for the local gentry to send their children to, and the local Catholics. My sister went there.

'Do you know that you have upset the Canon?' the nun asked in her lilting Irish voice. 'You know that your sister only goes to the convent because you serve on the altar? If you don't serve on the altar we would have to think about what to do about your sister. You wouldn't want her to leave the convent, would you now? Why not go to the Canon and say you are sorry?

You'll go to the Canon and say you're sorry now, won't you? And that'll be an end of it.'

So, I went to the Canon and said I was sorry. That is when it happened, again.

*

I stumble into the bedroom. I knock my leg against the bed. The door does not close. I hear a zip. I get pushed onto the bed, onto the clean white linen sheets. Its surface repels my face. My head is held down, fingers splayed across my ears my nose as I turn. I smell musk. The hand is removed, my trousers tugged down, awkward, with my pants. An oath. I am scared. I bury my head in the white folds of the linen. My hands lie useless at my sides. Then I struggle, but only to catch my breath. I feel it. I feel him. Inside me. Two bodies wrench in a Sussex chamber. Tenets of a new theology of violation are created. I see only white. I feel only blackness. I feel only my own hot breath, asphyxiating. Then it stops. But it doesn't stop for me. Not then, not now. Not ever.

*

There is a limit to evil, though it may not feel like there is. There is a limit to how we can comprehend evil, which comprehends evil, although it may not seem so. In *She*, Rider Haggard creates a subterranean world in which 'She, who must be obeyed' has complete control. It is an empire of evil, of the mind, seemingly all-comprehending. But outside that dark world, not a hundred miles away, the British Empire is conducting itself, with all its compromises, bringing civilization to the uncomprehending world, the glory of the West to the heart of Africa.

As a statement, that is not so simple or lacking in complicity than it might seem. There is no dark heart of Africa, and the glory of the West is not as innocent as we might hope. Everything is compromised in the end. All are complicit. Sussex is not the dark heart of Africa, but it is not a million miles away from it, either. In Sussex there are subterranean worlds, hidden from the glory of the West, where there is a limit to evil. I lived at its limits.

*

What happened to me is not unusual. I am not unusual. It has taken me many years to learn this. There is in what happened to me a kind of architectural beauty, a musical perfection. It has in it the germ of a narrative completeness. Fogarty was 'in' me in a physical sense, but he was also 'in' me in a psychological sense. There was something full and all invasive to his violation of me which it is almost impossible not to admire.

*

I am now going to make a statement.

> The first time Canon Fogarty saw me naked was when I was eleven years old at the beginning of September 1987. My family had just moved to Midhurst in Sussex from Dorset and the Canon came to bless the house while I was getting changed. He came up to my bedroom and encouraged me to continue to get changed from my school sports kit into my home clothes. He sat on my bed and watched as I changed. I had never met him before, but he had told me that he was our parish priest and that he had come to bless the house, and that there was nothing that I could show him that he had not seen before.
>
> Soon after we moved to Midhurst I became an altar boy and Canon Fogarty offered to help me with French and Latin after school. I would have to sit next to him and he would

place his left hand on my leg and sometimes further up than I was comfortable with. I would try to remove his hand but he would then reach for my genitals and laugh as he fondled them, sometimes undoing the zip on my trousers and actually touching them. I did not report this as he was a figure held in great esteem in the parish and I was embarrassed by his activity. Later he took to fondling my genitals on a regular basis, a price I thought I had to pay for my tuition, which diminished in its extent as he became more interested in me as a sex object. There are two windows in the study/sitting room of St Mary's Presbytery and the Canon would make sure that those at the back, which had no net curtains, would be closed. Those at the front he would pull almost to but not close entirely.

Some time after I reached puberty at about the age of twelve, Canon Fogarty started to question me about my sex life and sexuality. He would explain how to masturbate and occasionally to my great embarrassment and disgust, he would get me to masturbate in front of him to show him that I was doing it right. He would then help me to clean up and once took me to his bathroom upstairs to clean me up properly, as a boy should after each emission, that is, pulling back the foreskin and squeezing all of the semen out of the penis. It was then that he showed me his extensive collection of pornography, which had titles such as *Hommes International* and which were extremely explicit, in fact, hard core. After each of these occasions, Canon Fogarty would take me downstairs and make me make my confession of what had just occurred. This took place on the hard-backed sofa in the presbytery, on which we two would sit side by side. Sometimes when I arrived for my tuition I would try to sit on one of the armchairs but there would be a discussion – quite good-natured – until I had moved to the sofa next to the Canon. It became ritualistic and I had no one in whom I could confide, my father being often away at sea and my mother a very religious person. I could not tell any of my friends, but expected that the same sort of thing happened to them too. Canon Fogarty made it plain that my sister's place at the local convent school, St Margaret's, very much depended upon my complying with his wishes.

All this time I served on the altar and soon also took up the job of mowing the lawns of St Mary's Presbytery. I would be assaulted almost every time I did this.

Before my thirteenth birthday, Canon Fogarty started to provide me with homosexual literature to read and to talk to him about. He would reminisce about his youth in Rome and demonstrated ways in which men could have sex with each other without it being a sin. This involved taking off one's clothes and rubbing vigorously against one another. He explained that this was how priests could have sex and yet remain celibate.

About this time our visits to his bedroom became more frequent and the Canon would fellate and rim me, neither of which activities I enjoyed and which disgusted me. From the age of nearly thirteen Canon Fogarty started to give me a couple of glasses of sherry before we went upstairs and it is around this time that I recall being raped for the first time. This began as anal penetration with the hand and led to full-on bareback sex. Often these sessions would be accompanied by explicit material. Occasionally, the Canon would fulfil his desire with mutual masturbation, which I would try to resist, but he was very insistent that it was natural and that other boys my age engaged in it. I very much admired an older boy: the effortlessly hip William Samson. He was the sharpest guy around. I asked the Canon if he did this with William; he said never to discuss it with him, but strongly implied that he did.

The Canon was on the canon council of the diocese and would discuss with me sexual matters on which he was the bishop's legal advisor. Obviously I assumed that somehow Cardinal Cormac Murphy-O'Connor sanctioned what was going on. Also, the Canon owned shares in an Irish bank and implied that one day he would give me one of these shares if I cooperated, something that impressed me. I was also impressed that he read the *Daily Telegraph* each day.

I have no memory of the Canon's genitals or pubic hair, although I seem to think that the latter was white. Sometimes the Canon would say that I needed a full inspection to make sure that I was clean and this would involve examining my genitals and my anus. On such occurrences he would merely masturbate himself. One thing I found peculiar is that he enjoyed watching me urinate and would clean my genitals afterwards. The Canon taught me to shave as my father was away at sea and I lived in a family of women.

I have mentioned my friends. The Canon would insist on knowing all about their sex lives and what I knew of them. He was particularly keen on knowing whom I found attractive and describing them in detail. He would ask me to describe their genitals and get me to procure pornographic magazines from them for him. He would talk to me about my friend Michael Rugby, a fellow altar boy. This boy was the first person to mention the Canon's pornography to me. By this time, I was so inured to the experiences that took place in St Mary's Presbytery that I did this, once obtaining a copy of Alan Hollinghurst's novel *The Swimming-Pool Library* for the Canon to read, a book he found to be dull in the extreme with its lack of intercourse. He was particularly keen on images of erect penises and would show them to me at any opportunity. This would normally lead to a sexual assault.

When I was fifteen, I tried to leave the Church. I was very confused and disgusted both with the Canon and myself, and by what had and was taking place, but I was assured by the Canon that although it could not be talked about, it was perfectly normal. The Canon sent a nun – I think Sister Jerome or Mother John perhaps – from the convent to tell me how upset he was and to remind me that my sister's place at the school was in the gift of the Church, the school being private. This forced me to return to my activities as an altar boy, gardener and sexual partner, albeit an unwilling one. After approximately three hundred sexual activities, I eventually thought that I had had enough and had to leave Midhurst. For this reason I applied to Sherborne School in Dorset and won their top scholarship. This enabled me to get away from the Canon and I gave up attending Church, as Catholics were allowed to do. At this time the symptoms of my mania – I have bipolar I disorder – began to manifest themselves and I became obsessive. I was living in an all-boy house and yet had no one with whom to share my experience. I therefore attempted to commit suicide by taking an overdose of medication. I only survived because the scout found a tablet under my bed and so they were able to save my liver. When the Canon heard about this, he drove down to Sherborne and gave me £50 not to tell anyone about anything that had happened between us. I had to leave the school for the remainder of the year. After a period living in an Anglican commune called Pilsdon Manor near Bridport, I returned to my parents' house in Sussex. I discovered, to my horror, that the Canon had arranged for me to see a psychologist: his former parishioner Dr David Chance. This doctor would not believe my stories about the Canon and after a few sessions I ceased to attend.

Returning to Midhurst was not easy. I had to walk past the presbytery to get into the town and the symptoms of my disorder had worsened considerably. It has been suggested to me by a number of eminent psychiatrists, including my current psychiatrist, Professor Charles Timmins, Anstruther Professor of Psychiatry of the University of Oxford, that the events of my teenage years may have triggered my disorder. I have since been on strong and experimental medications and attempted to commit suicide a number of times, most recently when I read about the Canon's stroke, paralysis, and inability to communicate in the parish newsletter. I eventually decided to tell my parents and sister what had happened because my life was falling apart at the moment of its greatest triumph. I had just been appointed Junior Research Fellow at University College, Oxford, but things were becoming very strained at home. I don't think I will ever understand what happened to me nor how I couldn't get it to stop, but it has estranged me from the Church and almost from my family. My disorder has had a near-devastating effect on my life and it is only now with the correct medication and weekly psychotherapeutic support that things are slowly beginning to improve. I still have a severe distrust of people and can go out only when I am accompanied. The University of Oxford is having to make many adjustments in order to accommodate me and my behaviour and it will be difficult for me to find a permanent and suitable career, and that which I have found I excel in has been interrupted with loss of earnings, as well as spiritual loss. The incidental expenses of taking time out, paying for psychiatric and psychotherapeutic care and living at home and abroad without an income have been considerable, as have the personal costs, such as never having had a relationship or even not bearing to be touched; I thank whatever there is to thank that I have such an understanding family and group of friends who have lived with me and my disorder for the past twenty-five years.

*

There is something magnificent in the scale of Fogarty's achievement. He managed to make something eternal captive in the moment. At the moment of the most extreme and sustained violation and abuse, he managed to make a spiritual deed of a physical one. There are two ways of saying the word confessor in English, and both of them mean rape to me. The man to whom one confesses and the act of confession, each and both are contained in that one word: confessor, rape.

*

Why are there hardly any voices in this book? A great deal was said, discussed. But voices fade while their wisdom flares into a brilliant maturity, a mode of living. It is not the voices I remember, although I honour what they said in my thoughts and works and deeds. For all that, it was gaining a voice, going to the police and discussing my past that saved me. I am a man of the written word, a scholar not an actor. My voice can't be heard, elided as it is by the detachment of a scholar. Strange, then, that in my work I give voice to the past, the dead, the brilliant, with a mind to what was unsaid, saying what was not written, the silent voiced, understood at last by an unknown young man in another age in an Oxford library. Surrounded by the fineness of the Bodleian Library's august architecture, the confidence of the sixteenth century is made to speak down the generations. The letters of the seventeenth century, the joy and intelligence of the eighteenth are allowed to say to posterity what they could not say to their presents: that they endure, which they did not know they would.

Why does Fogarty scarcely have a voice? Why does he only speak the words of a priest? Surely there is something to be learned from all those hours of words, that persuasiveness, in the pulpit and in the presbytery?

I choose not to give him a voice. To me, the words all meant nothing, were just that, words, so many words. Rhetoric that took a child and would have destroyed him with its insistent, rhythmic, plosive-suasive penile aggression.

Fogarty cannot have a voice in this book, because he is not convincing, although he convinced me then. He spoke in a measured, ordered way, with a voice that led to irrefutable conclusions.

But in my book almost all voices are silenced, to permit me to speak. The rabble of conversation dies and a simple truth speaks out. In the hurry of conversation, my friend Henry, who was the first to know what had happened to me before we met at Sherborne, said to me years ago that my autobiography should be called *Let's Not And Say We Did*. That no longer obtains. We Did. He did. Fogarty did. Let's say that he did.

★

I was only a child, a boy. The problem with childhood rape is that it smacks of the juvenile. Child abuse is wasted on the young.

*

'Facio. Facis. Facit. Facimus. Facitis. Faciunt.'

We are seated in the study of the presbytery in Midhurst. We have been at our studies for half an hour. We have been at our studies for weeks. It is fast work. We are good at this. I am good. He is good. They are good.

He takes my hand.

'Facio. Facis. Facit. Facimus ...'

He squeezes my hand. He moves our hands around between us, as if thinking. I am thinking. He is thinking. They are thinking.

He places our hands in my lap and moves them against my groin, rubbing. I am anxious. He is anxious. They are anxious.

He squeezes my hand and rubs my genitals through my trousers. Then he lets go of my hand. Relief. Breathe.

Then he moves his hand into my groin. He fiddles with my trousers. I have a sinking feeling in my stomach, and in my groin. Not now. Not again. My penis retreats into itself in my trousers. I feel it shrivel.

His hand has undone my zip. I am undone. He is undone. They are undone. His hand enters my trousers. He squeezes my penis and rubs it. I dare not look at him. I look at the small gap in the curtains. The light outside scarcely enters the darkened room. On the wall St Peter's Basilica looks formidable. The power of the Church! How it endures.

I am aware of the rubbing in my trousers and, without wanting to, I am responding. My penis is now semi-erect. I breathe. He breathes. They breathe.

Time passes in this study, now, in Sussex. Outside no bird sings. The light falls in a sharp shaft through the small gap in the curtains. The books of the library, of this library of a canon lawyer, stand by, useless, as the law is broken.

Some moments have passed. I breathe rapidly now.

Then it stops. My penis is released. It sticks out of my trousers, useless between us.

The Canon utters an oath. Gets up.

'Stay there.'

He leaves the room. I stay. I wonder. I hear him pass upstairs. Pass into his bedroom. The door remains open, at least he does not close it.

Time passes.

My penis shrinks. I remain, anxious, on the hard, embroidered sofa. I hear a noise upstairs.

I tuck my penis into my trousers, feeling not quite satisfied, and not quite satisfied. My breathing has slowed. I look up at the light and do up my zip.

I listen to the noises of the house.

Time passes. I sit deeply in the sofa, withdrawing into its unforgiving hardness. There is no comfort here.

Then I hear him, descending the staircase. He enters the room and sits down next to me. I do not look at him, but at the books in the library.

'Facio. Facis. Facit. Facimus. Facitis. Faciunt.'

I think of upstairs and what happened there, and here. At least we did not go upstairs (I think). Not that once, not that time. There will be others. There will be small satisfactions in this place. Small satisfactions.

*

What makes a good rape? You'd think intelligence, by all accounts, but that may be wishful thinking. It's not the gift of the literati. It's not unthinking though either, for all its animal qualities. I think a good rape has to be really thoroughgoing, both bodily and mentally. To do it properly you have to get into the individual in two senses. Was Fogarty a good rapist? By all accounts he had beginner's luck, but the Church doesn't like to show the workings out and perhaps he'd had practice.

Maybe he just had a natural flair for it. If anything, it was effective.

I am now forty, and these events occurred quarter of a century ago, which may not seem long but it is all my adult life.

*

Each day I construct the self. Today I construct the self. I wake. And the world is a mystery to me. Not wonderful, although I wonder at it, and at myself. It is like having Alzheimer's (I imagine). Not knowing quite who I am, what I am doing, what I am doing in the world. I do not know the self. From when I wake up I construct the self. Not every day, although when I am like this it seems like every day. I look for clues around me as to who I am and where I come from. What I am doing. What I am doing in the world.

My academic work is not a mystery to me, although my academic self is. I look myself up online and there I am: Dr Stephen Bernard, of the University of Oxford. Author of a number of books and many articles in the UK, and Germany, and the United States. So far away! And yet I am out there, over there, part of their culture, speaking to itself.

The Plays and Poems of Nicholas Rowe is the work of the past ten years, now complete. The work of many people, taking care and time to make it excellent, to make it important, to make the past speak to the present, again. I hold it entire in my mind. Even when I do not know the self, I know that. It is part of me, of who I am and what I do. I construct Nicholas Rowe as I construct the self.

*

I am not interested in rape academically, which is both true and an understatement. First there was Ovid, then there was Shakespeare after him: the Rape of Lucretia. Samuel Richardson followed. He had clearly forgotten his Shakespeare: there is small Latin and less Greek in his etiolated rape. In the twentieth century there is J.M. Coetzee. His character the jobsworth of rapists, crossing his 't's and dotting his 'i's. Edward St Aubyn is the true artist of rape. Clarissa Harlowe was raped by someone she trusted; Coetzee's rapist is a teacher; St Aubyn's rapist is the writer's father. This rape is for connoisseurs. Fine and beautifully expressed, it preaches to the converted. It promises much and delivers more. But perhaps that's the tint of nostalgia for me. Can I be raped better? I can only do my best. But a worker is only as good as his tools. Can Fogarty do better? Did Fogarty do better? That I leave to the reader to decide. He tried, bless him.

I like my rape to come with trust, but I can see why some people prefer it without. It's a matter of taste, for some the best rape comes, is sudden, a violation which comes from nowhere. For me, I prefer to know who and what I'm dealing with. Rape is a war won by inches. It's as simple as that.

*

It is eleven o'clock and the Library is getting into gear for the day. The American academics on research visits arrive at nine, when the Library opens, eager to make the most of their time in Oxford, but eleven is when the native scholars arrive from their colleges, having checked their pigeonholes and dealt with the administration of the day, the letters from the Master of the college and the Chair of the Faculty.

A few colleagues come in and nod politely. I'm distracted. I look at my watch again. Two minutes past eleven. I think I will go and have a coffee in Blackwell Hall over the road. I can come back to this later. Soon enough.

*

From Sherborne School I went to Prague and Paris to live, to be away from my family and Midhurst. I did not know what to do, having failed as an historian. I asked my old housemaster Peter Prior what to do. He knew immediately: to do what he did and read English at Christ Church, Oxford. I bought an Old Shirburnian tie, deep blue and red and gold, and a new pair of shoes, and thus it was that I found myself having tea in the college rooms of a Student of the House, which is what the fellows of the college and the college itself are called: Richard Penrose Negus.

Richard Negus was an old-school Oxford fellow. Without a doctorate, as they were thought somewhat vulgar in the middle of the twentieth century – they still are, although they are the meal ticket to an academic life, the life of the mind – Richard Negus had rooms in Kilcannon. On his wall was a single oil painting in earthy colours of a young man. It was our first meeting – at Peter Prior's suggestion he had asked me for afternoon tea – and I asked who the young man was.

When Richard Negus was a young Student of Christ Church – he had been an Oriel man – he lived in other rooms in the nineteenth-century Meadows Building.

Richard Negus used to sit on his balcony with his cello, playing to the nightingales.

He had had three friends, of whom the man in the picture was one. They had wanted to have their portraits painted, but they could only afford for one of them to sit for an artist. They pooled their money and drew lots. The young man won. He had his portrait painted. Soon afterwards he died, like T.E. Lawrence, in a motorcycle crash. Richard Negus had thus inherited the portrait. On the wall of his college rooms, Richard Negus had a reminder of the impermanence of youth, the loss of promise; this picture looked on as he taught generations of bright young things the literature of their ancestors, the language of Bede and of Caedmon.

It was then that I decided that I would go to Christ Church to read English; it would be some months before Richard Negus would decide the same. Certainly, I had a formal interview with the other Students at the end of Michaelmas Term later that year. There was no question that my Old Shirburnian tie had swung it; it had not, but the recommendation of Richard Negus's old student Peter Prior, and a polite, rather awkward tea, which had an air of happening in an air raid shelter – a protected space, encroached by dangers – had begun it.

*

As I am now, a young English fellow in an Oxford college, so was she then. The daughter of the Jewish refugee Oxford historian Hans Eisner, she was born to brilliance, to be brilliant: Didi Eisner.

Didi Eisner is to me a tallish, striking woman, who wears her radicalism with an assured dignity and the optimism of youth. An English academic with a genius for psychiatry. She is the change she wants to see. She was then what I am now, a young Oxford fellow in English, with all the promise and responsibility that that brings. A promise for the future; a responsibility to the past.

We met in her rooms in St John's College. To learn about Ruskin and the stones of Venice. To me, not being born to the stones of Oxford, this seemed at first at one remove from the main event. The fact of the University, with its architecture and history, was the end in itself. It took me some time to learn that there was a world beyond Oxford and its colleges, a history which had happened not always because Oxford was there. At

53

Sherborne we had been taught to believe, in our Oxbridge classes, that Oxford was the event itself, an end
in itself. Now I had Ruskin and Italy to comprehend in
my life. Didi Eisner was the gatekeeper to a whole new,
urgent and expansive world.

*

I am in Accident and Emergency. Someone found me
on my staircase. Paralysed and vomiting. A normal night
for the students of Christ Church, where it was possible
to take a heroin overdose and not be lost. But this was
different. I had done something to myself, taken too
much alcohol, surely, but also something else. Benzodiazepines. A lot of them. There is a rush and a modulated
enquiry. Can I remember what I had taken? How much
had I taken? The real questions would come later, but
for the moment there was a body in spasms, vomiting
air to the air of the A&E department of the night-time,
some way from the Meadows of Richard Negus, and the
polite discourse of promise.

*

How had this happened? Why had this happened? I
knew, but I was not telling anyone.

I was the Mendelssohn of suicides, dying young, dying brilliantly. My first attempt at sixteen was my Octet, precocious and studied brilliance. I was never to achieve such perfection again, partly through a weariness and a realization that it could not be done better, or done again in the same way.

At sixteen, late at night, in my bedsit study in Abbey House in Sherborne, I had reached a maturity that I would not reach again. I had been performing that Hilary Term in Sir Edward Elgar's *The Dream of Gerontius*. That powerful expression of the movement of the soul from here to eternity.

> I can no more; for now it comes again,
> That sense of ruin, which is worse than pain,
> That masterful negation and collapse
> Of all that makes me man.
> ... And, crueller still,
> A fierce and restless fright begins to fill
> The mansion of my soul. And worse, and worse,
> Some bodily form of ill
> Floats on the wind, with many a loathsome
> curse
> Tainting the hallowed air, and laughs, and flaps

Its hideous wings
And makes me wild with horror and dismay.
O Jesu, help! pray for me, Mary, pray!
Some Angel, Jesu! such as came to Thee
In Thine own agony ...

On such rapture was I to make the journey. I was not to
know that I would often take it, and never to know that
I had arrived. The Mendelssohn of suicide was to die in
that attempt. All other attempts a mockery of lost youth
and the suicidal ambitions of a schoolboy.

Beer, washed down with vodka, washed down with gin
and benzodiazepines working God's purpose out in a
young, convulsing body. I wanted to die. I was going to
die. I had been rushed to the school sanatorium, found
with an unexplained and sudden illness, in spasms on the
floor of my room. Unexplained, and no one suspected
anything. I knew, but I wasn't telling. I knew that if the
overdose didn't kill me, the toxins in my blood would,
leading to liver failure and a slow, agonizing death. I
yearned for a slow, agonizing death.

How long had it been? An hour since they found me,
plus eight hours since I had taken the tablets. But all that

was a distant memory. That sound comes again, that sense of ruin, which is worse than pain, that masterful negation and collapse of all that makes me man. That sound has something of the eternal in it, and something of the night, last night. What to do now? Don't tell.

Now I am being rushed in a battered Citroën C5 across the hills from Sherborne to Yeovil, to Yeovil District Hospital. They do not know what is wrong. All I have to do is to keep quiet, not to tell. The minutes are agonizing, the hours will be surprisingly dull, with nothing to do, no purpose except to say nothing and to keep them from hearing the music in my mind.

Surrounded by whiteness, and cleanness, and people wanting to live, I mark the time until I know I have been successful and that I will die.

A phone call. The scout has found a tablet under my bed in Abbey House. They do not know what it is. Do I know what it is? Had there been more? Had I taken some? Had I taken more? (Had I taken enough?) I prevaricate, but my body is racked with a dry retching and I am tired, so tired. I had not thought that this would happen. What should I do? Peter Prior arrives with the tablet, having borne it over the top of the Dorset Downs for inspection by the team at the hospital. They do not know what it is. Can I last out, last out to die?

Peter Prior comes across to my bed. I must tell them, he says.

What to do? I panic, but know that I hold the cards in this situation. Can I lie once more? If I can lie, then I can live. I decide to acquiesce. There is no other word for it. I was complicit in that failure, the first of many. I had been precocious, but precocity was not enough in the hands of an inexpert participant, grasping after death.

I compromise. I try to retain some dignity. I ask for one thing in return: that my family is not told. I am surprised to hear that they will not be told. I will ... but first there is business all around me. A comic friendly knowingness; 'I told you so' laughs around my hospital bed. A quiet re-assurance that what I have done is not a problem, that it will all be all right. I hear the music on the hospital radio and my memory of an insistent tune, of the song of the night before, silently dies, and leaves me to live.

★

There is no shame in not dying, I discover. Not dying is a powerful argument for living in the world. A teenage overdoser in a hospital bed in Yeovil has a powerful argument for living, and a power over death, over other people. I will be here, not here, again. In other hospital beds, at other times. In many hospital beds: in Paris, in Prague, in Oxford, in Sussex. Pursuing the realization of a dream, the power of the question of life in an examination in which no one but me knows the answers.

Now come other questions, questions of motive. No one has died, but there must be a motive for the death. Urgent, insistent questions. Again and again, this time more gently. Why? I know, but I am not telling. I am safe in my hospital bed. My family lives in Sussex, ignorant of the plaything that their son has made of life.

A day passes, two. I have visitors. My housemaster, the chaplain, my friend Jerry Hedge. No one is saying anything, but already the wheels have been put in motion. There is the question of what is to be done. I cannot stay in a state of emergency for ever. What happens next: something breaks, a promise. Somehow I am cajoled into welcoming my family back into my life. In this clinical environment there had been no room for them, but they remain a fact.

My mother arrives, in a flurry of friends, urgently conveying her in her ignorance and distress from Sussex. She is not judgemental, she only wants to reassure, and to be sure that it will not happen again. That is a promise I cannot give, but I give it anyway.

The chaplain has an idea, which spreads from person to person. A solution: Pilsdon Manor, the farmstead near Bridport, at the foot of a hill, where the boys of Sherborne go before they are confirmed, to encounter the vagaries of life, will become my home for the next six months. There is general agreement. This is what to do in this situation. The reassurance of the bourgeois encompasses me in its wide arms and offers me a home in which to rebuild my life.

My father flies by helicopter to Dorset, arrives at the Manor. Kind, but not enquiring. Reassuring rather, that all will be well.

There are quiet, tentative talks in the garden, and time spent in the chapel, with its modern stained glass and its carved quotation from T.S. Eliot.

'In my end is my beginning.'

Time passes. The Anglican Church does what it does and offers answers which were not the answers to the questions asked, not asked. I know, but I am not tell- ing. I return to Abbey House for a day or so, to collect my things. I take the few tokens of my childhood from my study and transport them to the Manor. I leave my friendships behind, but they follow after, visiting me on the South Downs of Dorset, wrapped in a thick veil of illicit smoke – a shared transgression among teenagers who have yet to find the strength of their will – while the schoolmasters pretend to look on.

Mrs Kathleen Stoughton – 'Matey' – the House matron sees something on the day I return to Sherborne, and it plants a seed in her mind which will not grow, because I will not cast the light of truth on it. She sees Fogarty in the yard, handing me money. How he has got into the schoolyard, or what he is doing, or why, no one knows. That money is payment for a lost childhood and years of lies and broken promises. It is the price he pays for a lie that poisons the next quarter century of my life.

*

We are in the bedroom, upstairs in the presbytery in Midhurst. I stand in the doorway, anxious. The Canon looks at me. I look back. Not now, not this once. He gestures at my feet, meaning me to take off my shoes. I comply. I am complicit in this. He gestures at the bed. I move towards it. He grabs my hand, squeezing it, moving it around in the air between us. This is not friendliness (I think). I am not part of this, of that. He sits suddenly on the bed and drags me towards him He releases my hand then pulls me towards him I briefly catch his breath in the air between us glancing at my face He stands up He pushes me down I fall on the bed awkward His hand reaches out covers my ear pushes my head down on the sheets An oath He releases me for a moment then reaches down towards my trousers tugs at them pulls them down towards my feet with my pants I am on my face feeling the boniness of his fingers then the boniness of him in me in me There is a movement of sorts of which I am part not part I am not responsive in this responsible for this There is more movement on the bed that bed I move slightly up and down the sheets with the rocking action an action which pains me There is breathing in the air behind me deep breathing then a release a relief. I lie on the bed, feeling the stickiness of the semen on me. Go and wash yourself now, then wait for me downstairs.

*

I think of Hattie, my goddaughter. Nine years old in her blue school blazer, with her fragile grasp of London, where she lives, and of the world. I dream of empires for her, empires of the mind, as yet unconquered, without aggression. I leave Oxford to her, I will give Oxford to her. I will divest myself of my kingdom and leave it to her.

Delicate, in a floral dress. I think of her eventual corruption, her perfection, and I wish her a kingdom other than mine, my knowledge. This is the child – *ecce puella, ecce homo* – will she see me, see me for what I have been and for what I have become, a young fellow in an Oxford college, a young man without innocence, but innocent in his love for a nine-year-old girl?

The innocence of the child. The ignorance and lack of malice in the child. The hebephile was a youth once too, learning that the body contains the universe of creation.

The hebephile loves youth, youth on the verge of conquest, of being conquered. He does not move on, unlearn the lessons of his adolescence, he lives them. Perhaps. Child, father.

*

I had read an article from last year in the *TLS* that morning:

> The Queen Anne period saw a vogue for the index as an instrument of political warfare, a weapon which cost one Tory minister an election, and which was ranged against one of Johnson's predecessors as a *Spectator* editor. The fashion for satirical indexes had begun in 1698, when the poet and lawyer William King contributed a four-page table to the second edition of Charles Boyle's attack on the King's Librarian, Richard Bentley. King's index, inserted at the back of the book, was entitled 'A Short Account of Dr. Bentley by Way of Index', and sure enough, each of the headwords relates to some aspect of Bentley's low character: his 'egregious dulness, p. 74, 106, 119, 135, 136, 137, 241', for example, his 'familiar

acquaintance with Books that he never saw, p. 76, 98, 115, 232', or his 'Pedantry, from p. 93 to 99, 144, 216'.

King's index is a rather wonderful twofold attack on Bentley – as Isaac D'Israeli once put it, it is 'at once a satirical character of the great critic, and what it professes to be'. Thus, part of its fun is that those page references are real ones. If we follow the reference to 'His Collection of Asinine Proverbs, p. 220', we do indeed find ourselves on a page where Bentley is accused of repeating the same proverb – about an ass – at two different points in one book. So the surface-level joke of 'A Short Account of Dr. Bentley' is that a reader really might need to check the details of some particular facet of Bentley's awfulness, and knowing Boyle's book to contain the material but pushed for time, be delighted at the provision of a functioning index. At the same time, the 'Short Account' is also a covert attack on Bentley for being an 'index-scholar', a pedant whose scholarship is based on 'alphabetical learning' – looking things up in tables – rather than a real affinity with the works of the ancients.

I am an academic, a bibliographer and index-maker. But, like King, my indexes are not only there to tell people where to find things, but to tell them what I think, would like them to find.

> Lintot, Bernard,
>> creator of the English literary canon, 5, 11, 12, 22–25, *etc.*

My indexes are an exercise in constructing posthumous reputations. They direct the reader to what is said, to be said, about an individual. They are careful, carefully thought out things, complete in themselves, insofar as they can be complete. Today I will construct an index to my thoughts, to my memories, to these paper cuts.

Am I a good indexer? I hope so, but that does not make me a reliable narrator. I am parti pris in the index of my own life. I cannot help this, everyone is. Everyone is partial to their own concerns, and the indexes to their lives are constructed not with what knowledge they have but with what knowledge they would have people know. The index is a secretive but public occasion. It constructs the self-constructed self. Am I a fine narrator? Am I a good indexer to this narrative of my life? Even my scholarly honesty and my good-natured frankness will not stop my prejudice, my prejudices in favour of myself, my self, from building an index which will tell the world of my illness, and the cause of it.

*

The beating heart of the Anglican Church gives me a strength to live again. A confession which is not my own. Through Pilsdon Manor, through Nicholas Ferrar's dream of Little Gidding and the faith on which that was based in the seventeenth century – which Eliot knew – I learn to live another life. Gone are the smokes and ruins of high Anglicanism, instead a simple faith of quiet reassurance that all will be well, that all can be put right, and all will be put right.

I return to Sussex, to my family, before returning to Sherborne to complete my studies. It is a time of learning, without learning. I have learnt to be quiet. I learn to lie.

I am not without my teachers. Fogarty has the powerful righteousness of the Church behind him and again reigns in my life. All my actions are controlled by him, my thoughts are controlled by him. What I say, what I can say, is delimited by this tall, dark man.

*

It has been a month now since Tonson published *The Campaign* by Joseph Addison (I think): on 14 December 1704. Oxford has been in ferment. This is a poem that will last, as the victory by the duke of Marlborough, which it celebrates, will last. This land has been 'storm-tossed' before, but in an age with less to regret perhaps.

> So when an angel by divine command
> With rising tempests shakes a guilty land,
> Such as of late o'er pale Britannia past,
> Calm and serene he drives the furious blast;
> And pleas'd th' Almighty's orders to perform,
> Rides in the whirlwind, and directs the storm.

What a year was 1705! This year (to me). In this year, this, the greatest image of the eighteenth-century baroque, tastefully turned out by a young Oxford Fellow: Addison, that quintessence of excellence. Youth, promise, poise, control and the making of the English literary canon – it was all here then, is now.

*

Fogarty arranges for me to see someone.

'What happened, Stephen? Why are you here?'

This is the voice of Dr David Chance, a psychologist whom the Canon has appointed to help me rebuild my life. I struggle for air. Now is the time to speak, for me to speak.

'Canon Fogarty ...'

'Yes, the Canon told me that you needed help.'

'Canon Fogarty has done some bad things' – I halt for a second – 'done some bad things to me.'

'What things?'

'Private things ... sexual things.'

'It's not going to be helpful if you do not tell the truth. Surely the Canon has told you to tell me the truth?'

I am aghast at the situation. The Canon has not told me to tell the truth, he has instead told this man that I will tell the truth, which is something quite different. These, however, are the tools I have at my disposal at the moment. This man, while my father sits outside, nervous at being in the world of professionals, wants to know the truth, but the truth is not what he wants to know. The truth is something else, something I must bring to the table myself. It sits on the table between us, unwelcome and offensive, toxic. It is a lie. This doctor does not believe it, he does not believe me. We are going to have to build a lie that explains things, that we can all live with, we are going to have to construct my illness, and that started in the surgery of a psychologist in Sussex.

Years later, I learnt about Chance, how he silenced the young men the Church brought to him. How he denied the truth of their allegations and made them ill, literally constructed their illnesses for them, so that they might live with the truth. This was the beginning of my illness, a truth built on a foundation of lies. Another self, found in another confessional, but answering to the blazing questioning of the medical profession.

*

Let me give an example of what happened. It's a straightforward enough story to narrate, although I am both the participant and the narrator, which complicates things. Man likes boy, man destroys boy. He didn't mean to do that, but it happens anyway. Society picks up the pieces. Perhaps the man pays for his actions, perhaps not.

We got good at it. We got really good at it. At the lies and the action itself. At first it was awkward, a first date with violation at the heart of it, but soon the participants learnt their roles, what they had to do to get it off the ground. There was a kind of beauty to the thing. First, the back and forth of getting into the bedroom – that was an art in itself. It seemed always that Fogarty was speaking lines he had learnt before. He had certainly prepared for it. What he had not prepared for was a refusal, but for some reason that he never got.

Then, there was the muttering awkwardness of the stairs. Getting from the classroom to the bedroom seemed a long way. A difficult thing to pull off. The physical obstacle of the stairs was always hard to navigate. One person eager to climb them, the other not, and not willing to enter into the spirit of the thing. This was an adventure!

The dread of the darkness of the bedroom. The whole action of this scene takes place in near darkness, with mirrors distorting the light. The walls a pale beige add to the mundanity of the setting. There is a dark pall cast over everything that takes place in this room that the faint lightness of the beige collaborates in, unwilling it seems, like the mirrors, to illuminate events.

The bed. Solid and central to the action. But this is not a bed of lovers; there is no nightingale singing out-side, only the lark. Something hurried, and painful, and awkward and full of meaning happens. Suddenly, in a rush of movement, and force, and regret – perhaps – another lie that cannot be said. This will be the cornerstone of many lies. Soft rubber soles murmuring on a carpet scratch their noise into my memory like ice plates cracking as the earth's poles reverse. At my back I always hear ... a fumbling, and a mumbled oath. I do not like oaths, I do not like the word 'fuck'. I do not like what it means to me. I like 'God damn' though. God damn you to hell.

A spot of blood on the sheets. How will that be explained to Mrs Findlay, the housekeeper, both of us wonder, nervous at the thought of her Irish eyes trying to piece together this action in the darkness. The curtains hang heavily at the side of the bed, blocking the light from this – wait! No. Go and clean yourself in the bathroom and wait for me downstairs.

Downstairs. I am seated on the uncomfortable embroidered sofa with its hard back, the relic of an age of polite conversation and a wealth that Fogarty's family has long lost. He reads the *Daily Telegraph* on it and completes the crossword in the morning, checking the price of his stocks and shares. Perhaps a cup of tea on the side table, while the oil painting of St Peter's Basilica watches over him, a memory of another time, of the English College in Rome.

He is a man of the cloth and in this room dedicates his life to the improbable rectitude of the canon law. He is a lawyer, with a lawyer's mind. After the sin must come the confession. I sit waiting for the judgement of Christ the Redeemer in the room, impatient to be off, to be away from this, with absolution.

The Canon comes down, adjusting his dog collar. He is the Canon again, in his dull black clothes. He sits down next to me and intones the words which will lead to the act of contrition, an act of attrition in the battle to silence the blank, uncomprehending, yet accusatory words of a child.

Better than the silence is the confession. The expression of wronged innocence, contorted into the matrix of the ignorant Church. This is not a true confession, it is not made with an honest heart, welcoming the love and forgiveness of the true God. It is something that must be said, again and again, as the acts it confesses take place again and again, over many years, a whole pubescent generation. This now is my reckoning.

*

O. O. mag. num. myst. er. ium. That thought again, that thought of my destruction, being plotted in a room somewhere, by someone unalone, in concert, with malevolent intent and urgency.

The paranoid thought. Think it away, gone. Concentrate on something. The drapery on Roubiliac's bust of Alexander Pope. As good a thing as any.

Think of the folds, the texture. Concentrate on it. Luxuriate in it. Think of the silk, the weft of it. Where is the paranoid thought now? I struggle with it, thinking of the drapery. It is insistent, but more indistinct now. And now, thinking of the beauty of the material, the artistry: gone. But the memory of it remains, like the bust of Pope, a monument to posterity of the complication, the complicatedness of the past.

*

I'm in the Languedoc with a friend. It is summer. We decide to take the little yellow train up into the mountains. On the peaks there is snow. Outside the white-green florid meadows chant their hymn to creation. A slow movement, carefully finding its way from Villefranche-de-Conflent to Font-Romeu-Odeillo.

On the train, in the carriage is a mother with her young son. I can speak the language of childhood, even internationally.

'Je suis né sur une petite orange bleue, sous les étoiles immense, aussi silencieux.'

I am not very good at this. The child looks puzzled and the mother pulls him close to her. The carriage, with its open windows and yellow doors suddenly seems small for three people and a child. Something of my own childhood speaks to me, speaks through me perhaps to these – these foreign people. I think I see through foreigners so, but at this moment it seems to me that they see through me, from the mountains of Languedoc to the heart of the Downs of Sussex.

My friend looks out across the meadow, ignorant of what I am thinking, of what I know happened to me, happens, is happening.

*

There is an exhibition in Blackwell Hall of John Selden's great map of China. It is a masterpiece. A wonderful creation, speaking of the limits of the world and days of exploration. At the edge of the known world there is a lack of conviction, a wonder at the unknown. Its colours are faded – how glorious they would have been! – telling the mysteries of the East and of a country not yet a country, pieced together from the fragments and memories of the Jesuits and the first visitors to that place beyond. I take a moment to look, carefully. If only I had the time, I would learn the names of these places, learn what happened there and when and why. But the day is impatient for me and in Duke Humfrey's Library my work awaits.

*

When I construct an index, when I construct an index to my life, what will be the main entries?

> Bernard, Gerard,
> Bernard, Helen,
> Bernard, Margaret,
> East, Henry,
> Eisner, Didi,
> Essen, Odette van,
> Fogarty, Canon Dermod,
> Johnson, James,
> Lintot, Bernard,
>   and the English literary canon,
> McFergus, Fergus,
> Mulgrave, Sunny,
> Normanby, Hattie,
> Normanby, Richard,
> Pemberton, R.A.,
> Repton, Anne,
> Tagus, Frederick Sanford, marquess of,

Last will be 'Bernard, Stephen'. I am not the most important person in my own life.

★

I am an ill man. It started when I was a teenager. It first manifested itself after my first suicide attempt. It was brought into this world in a surgery in Sussex. The existence of my illness was invented by a wicked man, a believing unbelieving man in the psychologist's chair. I would live with the reinforced truth of this condition for the best part of a quarter of a century, until I learnt to challenge my whole superstructure of existence. It had to start somewhere, however, and it started in the mind of a man of religion, with the tools of the psychologist, and a pathological need not to hear the truth.

By the time I arrive in Oxford, my illness has been made manifest, has manifested itself in a fact. I live for my illness and by my illness. I am disabled by my condition, I am a sick man.

Before Dr Richard Gipps, there was Charles Timmins, a man who struggled to harness an illness for all ages with the tools of the twentieth century. A good man, mature, humane and caring, he did not realize that psychology, a branch of the medical profession, had made me the person I had become. He listened, intently, but saw the illness as something to be treated, not cured. He did not know that what he heard, my statements about Fogarty, were the real illness, that the cause of all that had happened to me had been the creation of the illness. He did not understand that to hear me speak the truth – finally, as I had, incidentally to him – was the path to recovery, to a world beyond my condition. He asked the question of my condition, how could it be treated, not why was it there. That was the question that he should have asked, hearing as he did, in passing, the murmur, the whisper of the truth. Charles Timmins was not at fault in this. He had to hand the power of an almost redundant psychiatry, unable to challenge the truth of an all-encompassing, vital lie. In this insistent, but limited, dualistic, or con-fused and postmodern world, this good man perhaps could not see the limitations of his profession.

*

My late teens were spent in pubs and punts in Oxford. There was something about the self-assured elegance of Bill Godchester with a pole at the 'Cambridge' end of a punt which I could never cease to admire. He was the son of a Cambridge cleric, a friend of Henry East's from the Queen's College; a beautiful man with many reasons to feel comfortable in his own beautiful skin. They made an odd couple.

Henry East wore his radical conservatism with an ironic lack of irony. He was not the most important man in my life, but he is the most important man in my life. Henry has just always been there, not always there for me, but a constant presence, with his unconventional wisdom and slanty way of looking at the world, as though the world could be made straight, if all things were just put right – which is possible, right? The art of making the possible possible is at the centre of Henry's existence. I have never known a man with such an enthusiasm for the new. Living in central London, an officer of the Blues and Royals, with a ceremonial sword for state occasions, he takes the ridiculous and makes it mundane. It shows his splendid isolation from the present in which he would like, somehow, to live, if there is a place for him. Is there? I don't know. He seems to find a place. He is comfortable in his own skin, which from schooldays is all he ever wanted.

Darius Rex was my pastoral master at public school and had been an enormous influence on me there. I thought there was something exotic about him, not because of his Persian looks, but because he had studied at Edinburgh; no one else in Sherborne had, all having gone to Oxbridge, except the sports master, who had gone to

Loughborough. If only life were that simple, and that complicated.

That was the world in which I first met Henry, a fellow chorister. His rebellion consisted in brewing Turkish coffee over a stove in his study. He would huddle over it in his poncho with his fellow rebels, waiting for the doom of the housemaster to fall upon them. A cup of coffee was his answer to the world in which we lived. It was not all about the coffee I realized even then, but still! A cup of Turkish coffee.

*

I only ever once tried to kiss someone: R.A. Pemberton. He was the real thing. In his company I could feel no wrong. Sadly for me I could do no wrong either, although it would not have seemed to me wrong, not once, not that once. He was the ultimate public schoolboy, with a shock of dark hair nearly falling over his stiff collar, which sat above the body of an athlete. I did not then know, as it was not written, Stoppard's masterpiece *The Invention of Love*, but I could have told A.E. Housman a thing or two about unrequited passion.

R.A. Pemberton wanted to join the army above all things, which he did, to my shame. I helped him to do it. Not conventionally bright, he needed help to understand the world at large. In the school House he was master of all he surveyed, but the world beyond, Westminster and the United Nations, was a closed book to him. In those days in order to get into Sandhurst one had to know a little at least of the world one wanted to command. It was an admirable sentiment. I took this schoolboy out of the barge yard and away from his passion, football, and showed him the truth of the larger world, at least the truth as *The Times* would have it. Day after day I schooled him in the intricacies of the political universe, which seemed unreal to us down in Dorset, in a town that closed on Sundays, and where the latest results on the back pages were all of the world that concerned us. Slowly but surely R.A. Pemberton learnt the ways of men. He got into Sandhurst, but I never kissed him. That would have been to introduce him to an alien world without the compulsion to command, where boys could do no wrong, which was not right.

★

Bill and Henry were trenchermen at Oxford, living to the full what they lacked in academic brilliance, the wake of another age. It did not seem strange to me that they would wear finely made suits from Ede & Ravenscroft, the tailors to the Queen, founded in 1688 at the 'Glorious Revolution' to dress the movers and shakers under the Williamite dispensation.

Ede & Ravenscroft made the gowns for the University, those markers of distinction. It was a proud moment to be kitted out in their scholar's gown, to show to the world – at least a world that was unimpressed with less – that one had arrived at some mark of success. Always in that shop when I went to purchase carefully tailored jackets on my father's account, they would address me as 'Sir' and welcome me as 'Mr Bernard'. It was only yards from one of the busiest high streets in the country, but it was a world away from it, and from a different time. The unobtrusive till would not ring until after one had left, without signing for anything, something vulgar which only they had to deal with. It was a sad day for me when 'Mr Bernard' gave way to 'Dr Bernard' in their mouths. It was the coming of age of a generation.

★

How did I find out that Oxford was even more rarified than my dreams of it? The first October morning I awoke in my set in Peckwater Quad, I opened the tall, richly brocaded curtains to see, at 6 a.m., a solitary figure collecting the empty champagne bottles left on the lawns from the night before. So much champagne! It would start at four in the afternoon, after a light lunch, heavy on the beer, and carry on well into the early hours, long after Tom Tower had called in the students of the House with its one hundred and one knells at nine o'clock.

The first year I was in Oxford, I tried to commit suicide. I returned the next year, the same man, with the same problems and intentions. This time round, I shared my life with Freddy Wyndham, earl of Sanford, an old Etonian with a finely structured face, open to any new experience, and with an urban style borrowed from the precincts of New York. With Freddy I learned about the aristocracy and its unusual ways: estate-bottled mineral water for brushing one's teeth in – teeth that always looked perfection – bred of good pan-European stock. His great-great grandmother was Victoria, Empress of India, and his mother a lady-in-waiting. His house was on Hyde Park Corner, sharing a fox with the Queen at Buckingham House over the junction. High walls separated the gardens, but they had an ease of access to monarchy, present at the State Opening of Parliament, when Freddy, as a boy, neat in his red and gold jacket and breeches, would carry the Queen's train along the corridors of the Palace of Westminster, the seat of his fathers.

At Sanford House, as Freddy's home was called, there are Van Dycks in the dining room, and over the mantelpiece in the smoking room a solitary, weary Madonna by Michelangelo. There is an opulence and an extravagance in wasting the best of their possessions on those who are determined not to quit and to enjoy resolutely that simple, exquisite pleasure.

Freddy arrived on the second day of Michaelmas Term the following year. On the first day we less grand inhabitants of the college were treated to the sight of a maid in a maid's uniform and a capped chauffeur delivering the earl's essential possessions to his room. They did not look out of place in the college, however. Christ Church has produced thirteen British prime ministers and is accustomed to the aristocracy. That it straddles the worlds of the great and the good and the great unwashed is the result of its fetishization of merit, almost to a fault.

I have been kissed only once in my life, something I will never forget. The beauty of the University was Alice Heyshot, whom I idolized. We would sleep together, chastely, while outside men who thought her Zuleika Dobson would pant after her company. It was only natural that my place was taken by Freddy Sanford. Within a week of arriving he was her constant companion. I do not know what happened between them, but Alice Heyshot would play intellectual games with him, discussing Bacon, Berkeley and Hume, as was the wont of those unaffected by the weight of what they spoke about.

Freddy turned to me one day and kissed me. It was something I had not expected. It ruined all other experiences for me. I have never felt anything like it. That shock of rudely dyed blonde boyish hair and the beautiful face beneath it was something to know, intimately.

Now Freddy is the marquess of Tagus, on the long, stately progression to the duchy of Wiltshire and death. His youth has gone, but not his electric presence. I have not seen him in twenty years, except in *Tatler*, where he keeps the better sort happy with their happy lots. What it is to be born to rule! There was never any doubt in our young minds that Freddy had nothing but the best before him, or to doubt that he deserved it.

I remember the light that day, coming insistently through the dusty air into the oak-panelled room. It was hollowing out a space in the chilled air, the fridgidation of a place in which there has never been a need for heat, never been a lack of all that is necessary to live a full life. There is a riotousness about privilege, an intensity of belonging which all students of the House need to feel and which they feel long after they have departed those groves of academe. To be a House man – as members of Christ Church are called – is to be born to all that is good and right in the world. It is a sense of belonging which I have never felt.

*

Then there is Hardy:

> The boy strained his eyes also; yet neither could he see the far-off city. He descended from the barn, and abandoning Christmin- ster with the versatility of his age he walked along the ridge-track, looking for any natural objects of interest that might lie in the banks

thereabout. When he repassed the barn to go back to Marygreen he observed that the ladder was still in its place, but that the men had finished their day's work and gone away.

It was waning towards evening; there was still a faint mist, but it had cleared a little except in the damper tracts of subjacent country and along the river-courses. He thought again of Christminster, and wished, since he had come two or three miles from his aunt's house on purpose, that he could have seen for once this attractive city of which he had been told. But even if he waited here it was hardly likely that the air would clear before night. Yet he was loth to leave the spot, for the northern expanse became lost to view on retreating towards the village only a few hundred yards.

He ascended the ladder to have one more look at the point the men had designated, and perched himself on the highest rung, overlying the tiles. He might not be able to come so far as this for many days. Perhaps if he prayed, the wish to see Christminster might be forwarded. People said that, if you prayed, things sometimes came to you, even though they sometimes did not ... turning on the ladder Jude knelt on the third rung, where, resting against those above it, he prayed that the mist might rise.

He then seated himself again, and waited. In the course of ten or fifteen minutes the thinning mist dissolved altogether from the northern horizon, as it had already done elsewhere, and about a quarter of an hour before the time of sunset the westward clouds parted, the sun's position being partially uncovered, and the beams streaming out in visible lines between two bars of slaty cloud. The boy immediately looked back in the old direction.

Some way within the limits of the stretch of landscape, points of light like the topaz gleamed. The air increased in transparency with the lapse of minutes, till the topaz points showed themselves to be the vanes, windows, wet roof slates, and other shining spots upon the spires, domes, freestone-work, and varied outlines that were faintly revealed. It was Christminster, unquestionably; either directly seen, or miraged in the peculiar atmosphere.

The spectator gazed on and on till the windows and vanes lost their shine, going out almost suddenly like extinguished candles. The vague city became veiled in mist. Turning to the west, he saw that the sun had disappeared. The foreground of the scene had grown funereally dark, and near objects put on the hues and shapes of chimaeras.

He anxiously descended the ladder, and started homewards at a run, trying not to think of giants, Herne the Hunter, Apollyon lying in wait for Christian, or of the captain with the bleeding hole in his forehead and the corpses round him that remutinied every night on board the bewitched ship. He knew that he had grown out of belief in these horrors, yet he was glad when he saw the church tower and the lights in the cottage windows, even though this was not the home of his birth, and his great-aunt did not care much about him.

Inside and round about that old woman's 'shop' window, with its twenty-four little panes set in lead-work, the glass of some of them oxidized with age, so that you could hardly see the poor penny articles exhibited within, and forming part of a stock which a strong man could have carried, Jude had his outer being for some long tideless time. But his dreams were as gigantic as his surroundings were small.

Through the solid barrier of cold cretaceous upland to the northward he was always beholding a gorgeous city—the fancied place he had likened to the new Jerusalem, though there was perhaps more of the painter's imagination and less of the diamond merchant's in his dreams thereof than in those of the Apocalyptic writer. And the city acquired a tangibility, a permanence, a hold on his life, mainly from the one nucleus of fact that the man for whose knowledge and purposes he had so much reverence was actually living there; not only so, but living among the more thoughtful and mentally shining ones therein.

In sad wet seasons, though he knew it must rain at Christminster too, he could hardly believe that it rained so drearily there. Whenever he could get away from the confines of the hamlet for an hour or two, which was not often, he would steal off to the Brown House on the hill and strain his eyes persistently; sometimes to be rewarded by the sight of a dome or spire, at other times by a little smoke, which in his estimate had some of the mysticism of incense.

Then the day came when it suddenly occurred to him that if he ascended to the point of view after dark, or possibly went a mile or two further, he would see the night lights of the city. It would be necessary to come back alone, but even that consideration did not deter him, for he could throw a little manliness into his mood, no doubt.

The project was duly executed. It was not late when he arrived at the place of outlook, only just after dusk, but a black north-east sky, accompanied by a wind from the same quarter, made the occasion dark enough. He was rewarded; but what he saw was not the lamps in rows, as he had half expected. No individual light was visible, only a halo or glow-fog over-arching the place against the black heavens behind it, making the light and the city seem distant but a mile or so.

He had heard that breezes travelled at the rate of ten miles an hour, and the fact now came into his mind. He parted his lips as he faced the north-east, and drew in the wind as if it were a sweet liquor.

'You,' he said, addressing the breeze caressingly 'were in Christminster city between one and two hours ago, floating along the streets, pulling round the weather-cocks [...] and now you are here, breathed by me—you, the very same.'

Suddenly there came along this wind something towards him—a message from the place—from some soul residing there, it seemed. Surely it was the sound of bells, the voice of the city, faint and musical, calling to him, 'We are happy here!'

I know that. Have felt that cool, expectant, welcome, welcoming, begotten air from Christminster.

*

In that second year at Christ Church, I attempted suicide again. The roundabout turned too quickly for me and I fell off, back to Sussex and into the arms of my family. That is where I belong. On my final day, as the storm, correctly for the moment, clapped out its thunderous rage above the college, I walked with my father across the quad where I first realized what Oxford would mean to me. I looked up. In each window through the darkening rain I could see someone had arranged large, simple, white paper letters to spell out

GOODBYE STEVO BERNARD

I know we went back to Sussex after that, but I never really ever left Oxford again.

★

My twenties were known by my friends as my 'wilderness years' – even while I was living them. They were great fun, but not a time of great illumination. The most important man in my life then was Tom Scott, of whom it was always said with some admiration and justification that he was 'entering into a grand period in his life'.

Tom was my tutorial partner at Christ Church and a constant source of wonder. He lived every minute in an expansive way, selling a grand piano here, a picture there, to fund his extravagant lifestyle. It was hard not to be carried away on the wave of enthusiasm and euphoria that followed in his wake wherever he went.

A slight, puzzled man, astonished by his own capacity to live life well, Tom Scott was also deeply caring and solicitous for the wellbeing of everyone whose life he touched. In him I found a love of the absurd, which would be accompanied by an unironic and unapologetic capability to make the most of things: the quiet pint in the Grenadier in Knightsbridge, then lunch at Green's in Mayfair, as everywhere else seemed a little less than the sum of its parts. Each of these things and many more added to the vim with which he lived life. It was never dull. Quietly and unsurprisingly, Tom Scott became an accomplished banker, husband and father, and, without knowing how, had done what he knew how to do: to live life well.

Tom covered for my lack of scholarship a lot when we were students at the House. Never being afraid to brazenly elide the discomfort of an unwilling and unaccomplished individual beside him who didn't quite know why he was there – although Tom did – or how to get out of the situation. Anglo-Saxon seemed to be a second language to Tom, and he knew the joy of Sidney and Spenser, why they were important, and how. It took me many years in his shadow – and what a long shadow he cast over my studies in my thirties – to see that the secret of Tom Scott was he knew the secret to living life, to see what is good in the world and what is bad, and to make it better.

If only I could convey the joy of Tom Scott. Secretly, I have tried to be him, but I am not him and was not meant to be. His pleasure in the mundane, and in the brilliant, is not something I can share. I can admire, but I cannot make it part of me, of living.

*

I am in the American Hospital in Paris (I think). I am unclear as to why I am here, there. Something has gone wrong. A young, assured Jewish-American doctor with a friendly clean-cut face comes up to the bed. Looking like the Upper East Side but dressed like Paris.

'*Savez-vous ce qu'il a pris.*' [Do you know what he has taken yet?]

It is quiet. I look at the clock on the wall of the brilliant white ward, the electric light humming.

'*Est-ce qu'il est accompagné?*' [Is there anyone with him?]

So quiet. A gentle French hum of action and inaction around me in the early hours of a Parisian morning. It smells of medicine and cleanliness in here.

'Right. Let's have a look at you, young man. *Avez-vous son dossier?* [Do you have his notes?] What seems to be wrong with you then?'

This is going to be a long night. Another night, in another country.

★

The air is not so chill now as earlier in the morning. I have had my morning coffee, but I took longer over it than I should. I cross over Broad Street from the Weston Wing of the Bodleian to the Clarendon Building and under the august gates of the sixteenth-century Great Court of the Bodleian back into the Library. I must get on. There have been too many distractions today and the editors of the *TLS* want my copy by the end of it.

★

After that, very little for five years. I work in a bookshop, stacking shelves, ordering books for unknowing eyes to read. I do not take much delight in the stock of my trade, but I have a keen awareness that at the heart of literature there is a prostitute muse, bankrupt of all motivation but profit.

Years pass. I meet Didi Eisner one day. She had not kept in touch with me. Charles Timmins had said that I was ready to return to Oxford and I felt that he was right, but I did not know how to achieve it. I asked Didi Eisner. She answered simply,

'Apply?'

With some trepidation, I applied to Didi Eisner's new college, Brasenose, and after a series of rigorous selection interviews in which I discussed the internal logic of Sir Thomas Malory and the richness of Derek Walcott's transcendent Homeric vision, I was fortunate to be accepted.

Brasenose was to be a blessing to me, a home. I stayed there for ten years, each year piling on restraint and resolution to do better, to be better. Under the watchful eye of Didi Eisner – and the Dean – I lived quietly on biscuits and still water. I challenged myself to be the change I wanted to see, and I changed – boy! how I changed. I grew from a man into a man.

I began by assuming the worst-case scenario each week: that I would turn up to a tutorial knowing nothing. Everything after that was a bonus, and I lived for the bonuses. Everything that I knew and discovered found a place in my world, and in my heart. Literature was to me not yet the canon, nothing so formal and regulated as that yet existed in my mind. It was rather a gift that kept on giving. There is a richness to the weft of literature that those who find themselves in its fabric appreciate. I discovered the reality of literature, living the life of the mind. I worked hard and my hard work repaid me. Each piece of knowledge began to fall into an orderly place in my thoughts, to make sense of the world as those that write make sense of the world, with reference to everything outside the writing, at once.

Brasenose College is not like other Oxford colleges, with quad collating upon luscious quad. There is the main sixteenth-century old quad – the quad of Alexander Nowell, built by John Johnson – and then there is the neat little 'deer park' with the seventeenth-century library and partly Wren chapel – an early work – abutting it, limpid leaves of an ancient indeterminate tree hovering above. Finally, there is the confident Englishness of new quad by John Jackson – 'Anglo-Jackson' – who built the Examination Schools, and behind that the New Building, designed by Powell and Moya.

It was the quincentenary of Brasenose and I knew how to mark its passing. I knew an artist, Andrew Ingamells, who is without doubt the finest engraver of recent times. I knew that he was creating a new 'Loggan', a record of the architecture of all Oxford and Cambridge colleges. I telephoned his publisher and asked if Ingamells would engrave a picture of the college to mark this moment. I would of course be in it, in an understated way.

My collection of prints of the colleges of which I have been a member is complete, from Beerblock's Elizabethan woodblock prints to the most recent representations. It gives me great pleasure to have these pictures in my possession, but the pride of my collection is the Ingamells prints. I have appeared in two now – Brasenose and Univ – in my Masters gown, urgently walking to a lecture, and greeting an old friend and patron, Professor Daphne Steele. The view from my study window in these colleges is shown on the prints, so that I can see outside, even though outside is outside. There are the noses of Brasenose and the tortoises and martlets of Univ, standing alert to intruders between the panels of the compositions. I will be glad that when I am dead these images, which I created, will last, a memento of my time in this wonderful, giving place.

*

Years pass. Years of hard work and earnest discoveries. I study the letters of Bernard Lintot and find I have something to say about them. Lintot I first discovered because I liked the timbre of his name. The learning, the scholarship came later. I did not know he was 'Lintot' then, the publisher of Alexander Pope. He had been a subject for belleletristic biographies before I came across him. I found him his true place in English literature. It was a joy to me.

I had been puzzling about what to do in my studies. The Arts and Humanities Research Council were paying me to write about the English literary marketplace between the death of Dryden and the arrival of Pope. It was dull work, and I made it dull. I found, for the first time in my life, that scholarship was not the life of the mind, but of constructs and arguments. I wondered what I could find to stimulate and please me and discovered the bookseller

Lintot, the publisher of Pope, who made Pope the currency of the eighteenth century. He was my métier.

★

It is a fine autumn day, although outside the light is fading. It is my twenty-first birthday. I am at the clinic of Charles Timmins, in Oxford.

There is a pause in the conversation.

Finally, 'Congratulations,' he says, warmly.

I am touched, and I thank him. There is a pause between us.

'You are now a statistical anomaly ... You are neither addicted to Class A drugs, an alcoholic, nor homeless, nor dead ... From now on every day is a blessing.' He smiles.

I do not understand his meaning, but he is in a good humour and I thank him anyway.

Later, when I leave, I pull my light brown, tweed greatcoat closer to me. There is a chill in the air, as I walk back from the clinic into Christminster.

We are a small, compact family, my mother and sister and I. We do not have much, but we have enough, and we have each other, which is all that we need. My mother, Margaret Bernard, is the cornerstone of our house. Without her we would not hold together. Since my father died there have just been the three of us. It seemed like we would never be entire when he left us, but it was for the best. My father died of a sudden and massive brain haemorrhage on 14 January. The date I write this. He is missed, but not forgotten.

The day when I told my mother and father about my childhood, my mother lost her faith, her reason for living, and the reason she saw in the world. She could not understand how she had missed the signs. The simple truth is that they were not there.

When I was a small child my mother had a great trick to play on me.

'What have you done to your sister?'

'Nothing.'

'What have you not done to your sister?'

Then I would tell her everything.

She never asked me what I had not done with Fogarty, so she never got the chance to find out what I did. She therefore knew nothing and I absolve her now of all duty of care for me as a mother then. It is in the past and that, as they say, is another country.

My sister, Helen, is a remarkable and resourceful young woman. She has a genius for children, for caring for them. She is a nursery nurse. Each day she takes the responsibility of care from the parents who leave children at her nursery and makes the day better and fuller for the children whom she comes across. It is not something I could do. Children are allergic to me and I to them. I fear that I will taint them with my own childhood. It can be hard. Will I ever know the fearless, earnest love of a child of my own? I doubt it. This is not to say that this is not something that I do not want.

*

All this was achieved, as I said, with the guidance of Didi Eisner and also Eleanora Tennyson, in the fecundity of their intellectual awareness and of the right thing to do.

They were aware of my problems, none more so than Didi Eisner, whose lack of weariness in the face of an insurmountable and intractable condition betrayed her bravery and her bravery on the part of the underdog. I could have achieved nothing in my life without Didi and nothing in my work without Eleanora.

There is an unstated moral rightness about Didi Eisner which infects all who are lucky enough to come into contact with her. Her passion is for achieved potential. Everything in her life is geared towards seeing the fulfilment of the gifts of youth. Year after year she would care for and support me, with meetings, messages, and hope. It was a sad day when she said to me that for years she had hoped it would all come right, but finally had to accept that it probably would not. Even then though, her boundless optimism and resourcefulness broke through and she said, in the spirit of Beckett, to try again. Fail again. Fail better.

Eleanora Tennyson has a first-class mind. Of that there is no doubt. She too predicates her life as an academic on the achievement of potential. Her secret pleasure is academic brilliance; she admires accomplishment with the passion of the accomplished. That said, her passion is also for the underdog; she wants the best for the most disadvantaged.

Eleanora made me a scholar, what I am today, but Jim Johnson made me an editor. Being an editor is not perhaps something that one would choose, but it chose me as a vocation. Jim and I have been in intermittent dialogue in an intellectual way for a good few years and I have something to say: our best exchanges have left me wanting to think more about things, but I sometimes want to say something which has an almost musical or mathematical or architectural inevitability about it and can be definitive and complete in itself.

Jim is not a steely intellectual, although everything he says and does is suffused with his sharp, practical intellect. Jim Johnson shows in his words that words count, in his textual criticism, and thoughts about the literary marketplace, that words do not come from nowhere and are not created whole for the world. Words need careful nursing to enter the multiverse. Lintot was one such nurse, shepherding his flock of intellectual and publishing copyrights into the culture of the eighteenth century.

*

Didi Eisner once asked me whether I would ever do anything other than editions. In the first place, I don't think I have the largeness of mind or intellect to present an argument or a big idea. But also, there is something complete and definitive about editions which I like. For me, the monograph leaves more to be said, but the edition can be an end in itself: finished, polished, complete, exhaustive, and touching on ideas as a string quartet touches on ideas – as an exercise in containing within a form the elusive and uncontainable. I think this is something that comes from having a truly academic and always calculating mind and also something which is the result of being a single man and never having had a relationship. I have no lifetime companion except myself. I have arrived at a point where I realize that my constant companion is my job, not in the way that one is a workaholic, but in the way that I live the life of the mind in dialogue with itself.

I have to live in the world and publications are my public engagement with the world, but editions are something intensely private to me. I have found something that enables me to do what I want and which provides me with pleasure.

That's all. Just a few random ideas, which I hope will fill out your idea of me.

*

I have not yet mentioned my steadfast friends Richard Normanby and Sunny Mulgrave, who have been my safest harbour ever since we first clubbed together at Christ Church. They live their example, with kindness and no judgement. Discreetly charming, with none of the froideur of their class that so many have, although they have a certain sang froid, jointly. One of the proudest moments of my life was when they made me godfather to their first child: their daughter Hattie. They did that when I began my doctorate, which I date from her birth. Unlike all my other friends, Ric and Sunny come as a complete package, making each other whole. They give me insight into what a socialist needs to do to live in the world and to make it work better, for them and for others. Humble, in their own way, they have given me the confidence to think as a family man, with the hopes for the future and a nurturing approach to life which comes with having children present in it. Children are always a joy, and they have let me have a child in my existence, which smacks too much otherwise of the coldness of the library and the solitude of books.

*

I am in an ambulance shooting through the night-time of Prague, rushing my body, which is in dry, retching convulsions, to the Central Military Hospital (I think). I hope it is not on time. I don't want to make it, not this time, not again.

The radio hushes out measured voices to no one, while the crew speaks to the driver.

'Copak je s ním?' [What's wrong with the lad?]

The paramedic adjusts the blood pressure monitor on my right arm.

'Holka. Kluk. Pospěšte si, chci být doma včas.' [A girl. A boy. He's young. Hurry up. I want to get home on time tonight.]

The driver switches the sirens on, hurriedly driving through the unforgiving autumn night.

*

In all my work, in all my studies I have had the company of two fine friends and fellow students. Fergus McFergus and Odette van Essen. We were the generation which came after the politically inflected scholars of Oxford in the late twentieth century, of high and low and Whig literary culture. Fergus McFergus embraced the world of politics wholeheartedly and turned it upside down; if there was ambivalence, then for him there was meaning. He brings to his work a sense of the impossible delivered, the inscrutable understood, even where it was not intended. Odette van Essen communed with the women who sat beside the men of state, who guarded their tea tables from the male culture of the Court and the coffee shop. The sexualized text would yield its intentions to her understanding. We were not the golden generation, but we had gold in our hearts, at least for each other, to whom we were all in all, at least for a while. If we had to face the world, at least the world of Oxford academe, then we would at least face it together.

Lintot had a bad hand. Frankly, his writing is barely readable. In another age they took time to read what had been written but now we scarcely have the time to read what is printed, let alone thrown out by a hand without an eye to the future. We puzzled over Lintot's hand, the three of us. Those black dots of ink on an unforgiving page. Was L'Estrange's edition of Josephus a 'bad one' or a 'sad one'. It was hard to tell, and reading his Josephus did not tell you much more. We laboured over Lintot's hand as he had not. Slowly we worked out that his five forms of the letter 's' were but a mockery of his minims, which tumbled from his quill like words from a child. It is important if we listen to the past to know that we are listening to what it said rather than what we might rather it said. This holds true right down to reading the hand of the past rightly. There is a great satisfaction to see what others saw centuries before us, clearly, as they did. That is the whole point of the textual editor, to get to the truth of what was said, how, why, where, and when. I have given the world Tonson and Dryden, Lintot and Rowe. What remains to be discovered in their hands I cannot guess at. If I have failed in my endeavours, I hope at least that it has been a noble failure.

*

This is not getting it done (I think). I must concentrate. The Library is emptying for lunch, but I won't go to college now. I have to get this done. I sigh and start again, stop. Then start again.

Lintot's promotion of the works of Alexander Pope ...

*

I have a small line of red dots on the back of my left hand, where the needle goes in. I have had hundreds of ketamine injections, more than anyone else, perhaps. The needle goes in, and the truth comes out. Sometimes I am a child again. Sometimes I have the innocence of a child, but I am not innocent. I know too much. I have known too much. More than anyone else, perhaps.

Everyone thinks they know more than everyone else in my world, and perhaps in the world in general. It is a fact of my life that I have often been in a sense beside myself, psychotic. There is a strange compulsion that comes over the psychotic which is not familiar to the merely neurotic. There is an insistent truth to the thoughts of the psychotic, independent of the real world. All-consuming, these thoughts overwhelm me and convince me of their truth. Having a logic of their own, they refract and distort the world around me, so that although recognizable to others, it makes no sense to them. The logic of the paranoid is something else to be believed, although it cannot be believed. It is a universe made for its own satisfaction, convinced of its rightness. The difficulty is to master oneself and the truth of the world from such a distinctive and unhaphazard perspective.

I am not Christopher Boone. I am not on the autistic spectrum. But something of Haddon's hero speaks to me. When Christopher sees the world, when the world crashes on him, a car crash of numbers with one insistent, vital number shouting out to him in the wreckage, that speaks to me of the confusion of the paranoid thought, a way of thinking which is known to the paranoid man. It is hard to see the one number which is important in the din of the experience, there is too much to compute, and chopped logic takes aim in the drive-by shooting of life. Haddon in this work is no doubt a genius, managing to express best what was neither often thought nor so well expressed. The clarity of his language and the beauty of it, the inescapable logic of the extreme, instantly lived, in the moment, is something to admire.

Mark Haddon reaches out to me in *The Curious Incident of the Dog in the Night-time* and Didi Eisner reaches out to me like Siobhan in it. The dog was 'curious' because of what it did not do, the noise it did not make, the unsaid. The unsaid by the dog speaks volumes to Sherlock Holmes, as I speak much by what I did not say in the past. What remains unsaid says a lot about us, as individuals. The love not uttered, the truth not shamed.

I do not think that doctors do harm, intend to do harm. Their whole reason is to see the world whole and to eliminate all that is wrong with it, insofar as they can. When you love cancer, when your existence is predicated on your love for it, what can they do? There is no reasoning with the paranoid, because they have their own totalizing reason. But there are reasons for this, and seeing that – perhaps for the first time – among all the half-truths and untruths of the perverted mind is part of the answer to its unquestioning rightness.

Doctor John Fortescue has an intelligent, questioning mind, open to the unknown, embracing experiment and discovery. Researchers in the US had shown that ketamine, given through a drip, could have a short-term effect, rapidly alleviating depression in people who had been depressed for years. Doctor John Fortescue had research funding to explore the safety of up to six doses. Charles Timmins, who knew of the work in the US and had been exploring the actions of similar drugs, referred me to the study. But the effects were sufficiently convincing in some people, including me, that the NHS trust supported Doctor John Fortescue in exploring whether the benefit could be sustained through repeated infusions, and then by giving it as a syrup. Unresponsive as I was to all conventional medications, Charles Timmins heard of this treatment and launched me into an experiment with ketamine, with myself, that was to have profound and, I hope, long-lasting consequences.

Ketamine works by blocking the glutamate receptors on cells in the brain. This causes the 'buds' at the finely ramified tips of the branches of the tree that is a nerve cell to rapidly grow, perhaps making possible, once again, the rich connections that have been lost in the winter of depression. It also boosts a chemical called Brain-Derived Neurotrophic Factor (BDNF) – which, to extend the analogy, is a bit like plant food. Ideally, they would like to see the buds take on a 'mature conformation' (i.e. a narrow stalk – like a leaf or a mushroom), as this conformation is more stable than that thorn-like 'bud'. But they do not know how to do this yet.

I began receiving ketamine injections five years ago. The effect of the drug was instant. It did not cure me of depression – or hasn't yet – but it altered my mind in a way that I revelled in. It changes one's perceptions, of time, of everything. Sometimes I would see the needle slip in, slip out, and think that nothing had happened, that no time had passed. Sometimes, I would feel the electric enervation of the Grand Unified Theory. Occasionally, I would scream out as Fogarty came into the room, but more often it was Margaret Thatcher. I could see her profile, you see, in the curtains surrounding the bed in which I received my treatment, and for an hour would be in the presence of an historical figure. It was comic to me that the great lady would visit me in my hospital bed, under the most unusual circumstances. It never crossed my mind to think that this was improbable and impossible. Her presence in the clinic was an honour, I thought, little though I then honoured her. Once, I was even visited by God.

I had the feeling that God came into the clinic to make his visit one dull Friday morning. I did not expect Him and He was not what I expected. A genial fellow, He carried Himself well for His age, I thought. He did not remain long, and I was not inquisitive after the great truths of creation. I was more surprised that He was accompanied by Margaret Thatcher, to whom I thought He might have had more to say. I can't remember what we discussed – probably *Star Wars*. He did not come back. Perhaps He was surprised at the reception He received. We don't stand on ceremony in the ECT suite of the Warneford. He shuffled off and was not seen again.

My greatest discovery during my pastoral days at the Warneford was that knowledge and understanding brought great comedy with them. My scholarship had always been tinted with, tainted with, comedy, not comic effect, but the comedy of a divine, benevolent resolution. There was something joyous about ketamine, its light touch, although sometimes its effects were heavy. Even when once or twice I thought I was being raped, it was done with good humour. The nurse would have a dexterous way of dealing with the situation, holding my head so that I did not shake myself into an injury. Sometimes the anaesthetist who sang Rossini in the clinic would break off his aria and wonder if perhaps the dose was not too much. The odd thing about ketamine is that it wears off in these cases almost instantly. The needle would come out and five minutes later I would be singing the anaesthetist's aria to myself, walking around the clinic with a renewed vigour and a spring in my step. I always left thinking that all was right in the world, even when I had been visited by Fogarty or by God.

The effect on me though was profound. I had seen God and seen that He was good. He was not what I thought He would be and, to be frank, I did not think Him any great shakes. I seldom told anyone of the company I kept. I knew they could not see my visitors. Are there any side effects? I would be asked. I thought it would sound odd to say none, but the presence of the masters of history by my bed seemed to me to be a truth they were not yet prepared to countenance.

Gradually, over time, Doctor John Fortescue adjusted the strength of my treatment, and I had no more visitors. I missed them, but they always brought dissociated, sleepy after-effects, which made me incapable of functioning well as I bustled afterwards round and about Oxford. A fellow, I would go to lunch in the Senior Common Room at University College after an injection. It was strange to me to think that only an hour before I had existed outside time, answering only to eternity and the insistent call of a bladder latterly incapacitated by anxiety.

Ketamine has perhaps cured me of my condition. I retain the symptoms of depression, the sleeplessness and the somnolence, but apart from those old friends and rivals, I do not feel depressed. Ketamine has brought about the conditions to cure my condition. The extreme dissociation I experience when taking it is the end in itself. It makes it possible for me to recognize the truth that my mood is just an unhelpful thought, not the visitation of the eternal. Likewise, my paranoia – yes, my paranoia, something I own, as I would my own child – can be cured by the realization that it is wrong, that the thoughts themselves and the reasons for them, their unrelenting reason, are wrong.

I had to ask myself a question: was I afraid of being cured? Doctor John Fortescue one day told me that I was now in the 'recovery phase', something I had never thought possible. What would it mean to me, what form would this recovery take? Ever since I can remember I have been ill. I owned that illness as my own, as myself. It would take courage to be well again, as I was when I was a child. I thought I had the courage to be a sick man, but the bravery that wellness would require was asking a lot of me. I had become a patient, needing patient help. What would it mean to me to be impatient for the day, to seize the moment and live for it?

I am a well man. Can I cope with perfect confidence, with the honest fact that there is nothing wrong with me?

*

Complication upon complication. I have a thought (I do not know where it has come from). That someone, somewhere is planning my destruction. It is as simple and as complicated as that. I have no evidence for it, but to my mind the heaps of evidence are piling up. I can be rational about it, but already it is convincing me, has convinced me, that it is the truth. Thinking about it is not the right response. Feeling it, that is not the right response either. I feel it, I know it. I know it to be true, that without any just cause someone is plotting my downfall.

What to do about it? Whom can I trust? Already it is seeping into my mind that those I thought I could trust are also part of this conspiracy, this conspiracy against me. I know I have thought these thoughts before, that they were not right, that I took medications and the thoughts went away, but that is what they want me to do, to take the medications and to cease to see through their plan, their plot to undo me.

I should take the medication. I have it here next to me, in my bag, in the Library. I always carry it with me, for such a time as this. It will take hours to work, but it will work (I hope). No, hope is not the right word. I can see the truth of the situation now as I have never seen before. I do not hope to know an untruth, for them to have their victory over me, for me to be compliant, them complaisant, in this situation.

Can I take the medication? I do not know if I can trust it, can trust myself, to make the right decision in this situation. Whom can I trust? I think of my mother, what would she do? She would tell me to take the medication. But it is poisoning me. It is making me not see the truth about the world, of what is happening to me. This is happening to me. Something is happening to me, and I can stop this.

I take the bag and go downstairs to the cloakroom. There is the water stand. There, in my hand, is the medication. Should I take it? I am only just now beginning to grasp the truth of the situation. To see entire and whole the overwhelming truth that someone, some people, everyone is out to get me. They want me to take the medication. I can see that. I want to take the medication, to believe the truth, a contradictory truth, to end this confusion, this complication, these complicated thoughts.

Am I rash enough to take the medication? It is what they want (is it what I want? What do I want?) I am alone in this room, although there are people in it, washing their hands, looking at me (are they looking at me?) I am very aware that now I have to make a decision, to grasp a thought among many thoughts (what am I thinking? I am not even sure of that).

Someone flushes the lavatory behind me, is coming out, into this room. We share a space, each of us aware of the functions of the body, but I am thinking now of the functions of the mind. I am aware that these thoughts, which press against my mind, trace their composition on the mirror in front of which I am standing. I see myself. I can see myself clearly, standing there, in a confusion of thought and alone.

The man passes out of the room and leaves me with my thoughts. So many thoughts. What am I thinking? (No, what am I thinking?) I am thinking a thought which is not rational, although it convinces me now of its truth. There is also another truth, that I am not alone in the world, that I have been here before and am comforted, helped by the medications in my hand. I make a decision. It may be my downfall, or the downfall of my self, but I take the tablets, individually, one by one. This may be what 'they' want, but it is also what I want, to be away from these complicated thoughts, this complication.

I look at myself in the mirror. I have done it now. Have acquiesced in my own destruction. If the minutes are intense, the hours will be surprisingly dull, I know, until the medication works, works its way through my blood-stream, into my mind, and corrects my perceptions of the world, which even moments ago was plotting my end. There is nothing to do now but wait, and already I am reassured that I have done the right thing. It will turn out to have been the right thing to have done. That I know, but I do not know yet. I know that there will be more complications in my day, in my life. I do not know what the day will hold yet, but I have taken charge, have let them take charge, have thought through, literally thought through those complicated thoughts and already I am more in control of myself.

This is not getting it done. I return to Duke Humfrey's Library. I must crack on.

★

It is past two o'clock in Oxford and an email arrives in my inbox.

'Acknowledgements.'

These are the acknowledgements for the Rowe edition, a work which has taken years, years in which I have lived in the eighteenth century. It is 14 January 1705 today and Betterton has a cholic and is not expected to last.

★

From the *London Gazette* for the day 14 January 1705:

> The French are fortifying Dezenzano. They attempted of the 22nd past in the Night to surprise Palazzuolo, another Town in the Province of Brescia ...

To the Duke of *Marlbourough*, on the
Trophies set up in *Westminster-Hall*.

For other Princes, let the Abbey be;
Westminster-Hall's a *Monument for thee.*

ADVERTISEMENTS

*‡ *The Peculiar Use and Signification of* certain
words in the LATIN TONGUE: Or a Collection of Observations, wherein the elegant
uncommon Sense of very near 900 common
Latin Words (besides the various Sense of the
same words) is fully and distinctly explain'd in
English Sentences, translated from the truest
Copies of the Purest Latin Writers. The Order
Alphabetical . . .

*

Acknowledgements, I think, are the means of tracking
the intellectual and personal histories of the individual,
of the individuated academic, in relation to themselves.
The lives of their minds.

An edition like this is many years in the making and there are many people to thank . . .

*

This is not getting it done. The literature editor of the *TLS* will be champing at the bit in anticipation (I kid myself).

★

You are not in fact a well man. That wellbeing is also a lie, also created in the psychologist's chair. Trauma can be the cause of psychiatric illness, and you have a psychiatric illness, it has a psychological cause, but it does not have a psychological cure.

There are not two minds at work in the world, a psychiatric and a psychological. No, there is one infinitely complex mind, which I find I cannot 'Print out'. I can see only the scars of these paper cuts. There is no simple solution to the questions posed in this dualistic/postmodern universe. This is not a failing in me – in us – but rather shows the limitations of the mind to understand, to understand itself.

★

One tablet, two tablets. Four tablets. Nine tablets. Today will be the day. Today will be the day when it all gets right. You can put it right. Swallow. The self. In a bottle.

★

One day my father died. It was unexpected; a leaden hand in a kid glove. He was there, then he was gone. His body lived long after his brain had been irretrievably corrupted. Did the doctors kill him with kindness? One moment we were told to return to Midhurst from the hospital in Chichester to get some sleep. We would not sleep that night. (Or perhaps we did?) By the time we had reached their home, it belonged only to my mother. We were told he had been given some morphine to relieve a discomfort he could not possibly have felt, and that was that. Smothered in an opiate chamber, unconscious that he had long been no longer for this world.

So, my father died and my mother bought me a flat, in Jericho, in Oxford. Jericho is the Oxford idea of bohemia, the bohemian life. It is there that they make the Turkish coffee of their youths, plot rebellion. *The Times* says it is a fashionable district, where you can 'see Mark Haddon'. I've never seen him here, but I know they are essentially right, that it is the sort of place that you would. Sometimes, in interviews, he says that he writes in a coffee shop, listening to the music of the eighties. You can, in Jericho.

My flat is almost a modern ideal of the typical Oxford 'set', although some say it is like an hotel. It has a study and a bedroom. There is no place to eat in, so I eat out, in a trattoria up the road from me. Everything in my flat is a brilliant white – the blinds, the walls, the sheets on my bed. It is a minimalist existence. The past hardly gets a look in, although there is one wall covered in eighteenth-century books, my library. I have there every edition of Pope and Dryden and the books in between, which you can buy at auction for their true worth, although I kid myself that I am buying bargains. The walls have on them a selection of prints of my colleges, with my precious Ingamells engravings taking pride of place. I like their clean precision, their regularity. All architectural prints speak to me from the confines of the ink on the page. There is something refreshingly neat about them, that they contain the perfect image of an uneven world. Oxford is famous for having a curved high street, which is the only imperfection I will allow the city. It is there too, on my walls, in pale grey and dull burnished yellow Ackermann prints of the sunsets of the Regency over Oxford.

My flat is also contained, adequate for my needs, which are simple. There is a television, unwatched, on one wall. BBC News 24 on a constant loop, only incrementally changing, is the hum of my study. Here is the site of quiet purpose and occupation. At my desk I send out messages to the other side of the world, about things that happened when first the high street was irregularly curved, when it had oak-beamed shops and coffee shops with fronts that spoke of its early medieval origins.

Once a week I will venture out of my flat or from the Bodleian Library to go snacks with Jim Johnson. Between us we have the intelligence to put the world wrong, and busy ourselves with fruitless but urgent enquiries into the facts of a forgotten world. Some of the most pointedly sharp insights into not much have taken place in the coffee shops in Oxford. Coffee, that cool rebellion against conformity, that radicalism of the bourgeoisie.

*

What's the time? I think I'll go and have a walk in the back gardens of St John's. I need a break. This is hard work. I have been very distracted today. Why do I let this happen?

I go down the stairwell and through the Proscholium into the early evening air. It is chill out, and the light is fading. There is Katherine Duncan-Jones going home for the night, having skewered Sir Brian Vickers on the point of her Mont Blanc pen. That is a case where two people see the same thing and see something completely different. It goes back years. One it seems cannot write without the other writing back. The mind in dialogue with the other. I wonder what each would do without the other. There is a symbiosis in that relationship. Two of the world's leading Shakespearean scholars, with two Shakespeares between them. Neither will ever be right, but neither is often wrong either. There she goes along Broad Street, back to Jericho, a drink, and Radio 4.

I follow slowly after, which is hard as she is not so very fast these days. Not like when she and Andrew Wilson went snacks with Iris Murdoch and John Bayley in north Oxford. I wonder if anyone will remember my days in Oxford, as I don't remember them, but index-like, as they may be thought to have been lived?

*

I reach the corner of Balliol and turn into Magdalen Street, past the Martyrs' Memorial of the morning – darkened now, though restored to its Victorian splendour

– and go into St John's. Sir Howard Colvin wrote an entire book about the Canterbury Quadrangle – the 'historian with modern views' – what a mind! To be pleased with fifty square yards, and delighted in it. I look up at the gutters which he writes about, and wonder at the workmanship of the seventeenth century. I walk under the statue of Charles I in his glory and out to the back, the immense lawns at the heart of Oxford, hidden in the city, hidden from the townspeople with their keenly felt disrespect.

The late afternoon. The trees are conspiratorial and the lights from the Laudian Library fall lightly on the grass. It smells crisp. I light a furtive cigarette, from my youth, and move into the shadows. A gardener is at work, or leaving it, his rake leaning against the crumbling stone walls.

I must get back to the Library. I leave, passing unnoticed into the early evening.

*

I am on Broad Street. Suddenly it comes upon me. Those racing thoughts, and a music. Loud beyond belief and insistent, pressing in my small, cramped mind. The lights are brilliant. But they keep flashing and then going out. That music.

*

O. O. mag. num. mys. ter. i. um. through these. critical. editions. these. critical. editions. one. dark. one. dark. night. O. O. mag. num. critically. Bernard. Lintot. made. O. O. mag. a choice of. great. num. and. lasting. O. O. importance. O. O. great. and. lasting. importance. in darkness. and. secure. O. O. by the secret ladder. mag. num. in darkness. and concealment. O. O. mag. num. fired. with. love's. urgent. longings. through. these. O. O. critical. urgent. longings. fired. with. love's. O. O. urgent. critical. concealment. dark. night. O. O. critical. urgent. longings. mag. num. mys. ter. i. um.

*

I pass Matthew ap Gryffyd on the stairs in the Library. We do not have time to chat, although we have time for each other. Always. We pass in the early evening, each busy with our work. The Library is not a place for friend-ship.

I think about Matt ap Gryffyd. One of my closest friends. A keen, intelligent, questioning, fresh, alert mind. Always open to the new in a constructive way. The only other disabled person I know in the University. He has an eye condition, a genetic condition which only he and his mother have in the UK. Doctors like him, they like his eyes. They like his genes. I like him, down to his genes. And I like his eyes too. Kind, intelligent eyes. Eyes of perfect friendship and acceptance.

This is not getting it done.

*

Five o'clock. I said I'd submit it by the end of the day, today. I wonder if they mean by the end of today? They'll probably leave the offices at London Bridge Street at six, but I could get this to them before the Library closes tonight. The wonder of the web! Malone's letters would have taken almost a day to reach London from Oxford. But for me: click.

I see the Keeper of Western Manuscripts in the Bodleian, behind his neat, quiet, orderly desk in Duke Humfrey's Library. He seems to know all the things deposited in his care, as they have been in the care of the Bodleian for centuries. He has an immense, humanistic knowledge and understanding. He is answering the phone now. Another academic calling in the night from Australia with an urgent question about the letters of Anne Finch. He knows the answer, but he is feigning ignorance. He is somehow, among all his papers, among all the papers in the Library, bored today. He will play with this person, but kindly and courteously, to pass the late hours of the afternoon, until he can go off, away from his possessions, not his possessions, into the night.

I must crack on.

> *... yet these efforts would have been meaningless, in the long run ...*

★

My personal and intellectual history begins that day, 8 September 1987. Before that little. A toy here. A face there. The son of the Dock Road in Liverpool? He was suppressed. I'm no Romantic, finding in innocence the truths of ages. Few memories as I say. But I miss nothing. You can't remember what you've forgotten. Paris. Prague. London. Those cities are my hills, my mountains.

★

After twenty-five years of painful ignorance of the world around me, although living in it, and living in it well, things came to a crisis. I was planning to be on the Continent for a conference, but found myself planning how to return from that conference when everything fell apart. Repatriation is not the best plan to have for an international excursion.

I was confused. I spoke to my friend Annie Repton on a telephone line urgent with need. What should I do? People don't often tell me what to do, I decide for myself. But under the circumstances Annie told me what I wanted and did not want to hear, that I should go home to Sussex, to my mother.

In the *Times Literary Supplement* that week, there had been a review of Cardinal Cormac Murphy-O'Connor's apologia. His justification for his actions, not to his God or even to himself, but in the court of common opinion. He was found wanting. The review told of a case in which a man had spoken to the two laws – that of the Church and that of the state – and had died by his own hand. How I knew how he had come to that end in such unaccommodating circumstances.

I wanted to die, but although all reason told me I must, that I must rejoin the suicide club and this time pay my dues, friendship spoke out to me and offered me the reason of love and respect.

I decided then to go to the police, but not yet. To involve the state in my actions, which had gone undetected in the world for too long. Years earlier I had had a similar violent response to the news that Fogarty had had a stroke. From my long experience of my own father's stroke and its debilitating and humiliating effects – which my father had faced with courage and determination – I knew that now was the time to strike. I went to the Church and made my complaint against him. Was I believed? I do not know. I did not care to be understood simply, I cared to be believed.

One morning, before my father's nurse arrived at my parents' house in Sussex, I went downstairs and waited. I waited for my mother to come down. At six o'clock on that spring morning, I sat her and my father down and told them something of what had happened. My mother and father had their own religious convictions, but this shook them to their foundations. In their different ways they were both deeply religious. My father retained his faith, but at that moment my mother lost hers. I offered her instead a theology of the individual child victim, a sorrow which could not encompass the passion of the Catholic Church. Only when my father died would my mother return to the Church, once, for his sake. At that moment my own words carried their own metaphysical meaning, the meaning of a child wronged, which overwhelmed the truths of institutionalized religion.

Fogarty declined over the following weeks, sometimes rapidly. The child protection officer in the diocese kept me informed, as my family and the Church waited for me to pounce, to report Fogarty's crimes to authority beyond their reasoning. Would I go to the police, and speak out against this man who had done me such harm? He lost his movement, then he lost his voice. Silenced, I could not accuse a dumb man before the courts. Dying, I could only leave him to the judgement of a God in which he had robbed me of belief.

Fogarty died. He took with him my chances of vengeance, but my work told me of the meaning of reputation. I would leave judgement to his God, but disgrace him in the eyes of the world. I would soil his grave, and deny him the bleaching agent, the power of a posthumous existence in the world. I excoriate and denounce him. Now, for ever.

*

There was at this moment in time the deliberate heaviness of a metal gate closing on my past. Fogarty had had his chance in this moral world and lost it to the throes of a logic which I could not understand. At times, I tried to understand it, its perverse, mind-altering alienation from all that is right. But that understanding was beyond me, I could only ask for redemption.

I have a voice now. I speak only the truth, and the truth is the overarching logic of unconditional love, free for all, free from the ensnaring aggression of an abusive, forbidden, penile passion.

*

Anne Repton. Annie Repton. Dr Annie Repton. A truly good character. Not moral like Didi Eisner, but good. Whole. Entire unto herself. I met her at Christ Church and have lived my life with her, shared my life with her ever since. She is my controlling angel. A pure voice telling me what it is to be a good person in a naughty world. The chronicler and editor of Charles and Mary

Lamb. She lives with the Romantics, with whom I have no, can have no intercourse, in a world of the intellect and imagination which is beyond me, which I cannot understand. It is my greatest failing as a student of English literature that the Romantics of the first and second generation are lost on me, to me. There is something about their emotional register which I feel alienated from. No, give me the peace of the Augustans any time.

*

I am aware of a noise, slight and muffled somewhere near me. I look up. I look around. There is someone settling down at the desk beside me in the library and, suddenly, I am aware of something else. Something has happened, somehow. I am beside myself. Literally beside myself. Some inches to the left of me, I am seated at this desk. I catch the thought in my mind. What has happened? This has happened to me before, I know. I have had the sense of being beside myself. What time did I take the medication? An hour or so ago.

It is as though there were two copies of Da Vinci's Vitruvian Man placed on top of each other, but not quite on top of each other. That is the sensation I have. I know this is a psychotic sensation, not being quite oneself. Something has happened in my mind. It is not even a thought, although it is manifesting itself as a thought. Somehow my self has been set at one remove from my body. I am aware of myself, sitting some inches to the right of me, of my mind. I am aware of my body, being there, not there.

Where am I? (I think). What should I do? The man beside me lays out his book on the desk and I feel almost on top of it, of him. He is not aware of this, but I am very aware of this. Of this odd sensation. It will pass, as it has passed before. It just takes time for the medication to work, to flow through my body, into my mind. But for the moment, for this moment in time, I am aware of being beside myself.

Maybe if I walk around it will stop, this psychotic experience. I get up. I can feel my body moving and me moving with it, but for the moment I am not in my body, but some inches to the right of it. It is awkward, uncertain, being beside myself, but I manage to control myself, to get from the desk to the door, from the door to the stairs, from the stairs to outside.

I breathe deeply and cross the great court of the Library, stepping out into the street. All around me the world is busying itself with its business. I can see myself reflected in the windows of Hertford College opposite. I am indistinct in the nineteenth-century glass, which looks corrupted, an idea of perfection not quite realized. I am clearly not beside myself, although that image of a man, of me, seems to me to be only part of the truth, of the truth of what is taking place at the moment.

I take out a cigarette and try to feel my way back into my body as the smoke courses down my throat. Breathe. Inhale. Exhale. Inhale. Exhale. Where are you now? In your body, but no longer beside yourself (you think). No longer feeling that psychotic thought. It lasted a while, but now you are entire again, for the moment at least. Go back into the Library. You have work to do.

*

It is early evening and my day's work is far from done (I think). The light outside fades, is fading. I am the light inside, fading. I stare at the half-bright, half-electric screen before me in the dusk-touched library and start again.

the publication of the twenty-nine-year-old poet's
precocious Works *in 1717 was to establish him*
as a bookseller of considerable importance in the
creation of the English literary canon . . . .

*

When I decided to go to the police I was addicted to benzodiazepines, my old friends from former days, with whom I was too familiar. Over time,
I found I needed their support, until their support
became unsupportable. I had given up diazepam some
months since, and the loss was keen. Now they were
only permitted to me in emergency situations and then
not for long. I needed them now. Doctor Fortescue
would call each day in the week before I attended the
station and ask my mother how I was coping. The truth
was: not very well. I knew that the coming labour would
give birth to a new me and I was edgy at the thought.

The one thought that had sustained me over the years
was this: that I did not tell the truth. The whole thing
was a massive, problematic lie. Now was my moment
to place the truth on the petri dish of legal enquiry
and find if it would be found wanting. On the Saturday
morning I was to attend on the police at the station in

Chichester, over the other side of the South Downs, I decided to make a point. I wrote out three times on three Post-it notes the statement:

> We have been brought up to love one another and to tell the truth.

I do not think that my mother and sister expected that with their breakfast. We passed over it lightly, after taking a moment to think that this was the birth pangs of a protracted labour.

*

I'm outside the police station. I have taken more diazepam than I should. Under my arm, in a feeble plastic bag I have my statement. Twenty-seven pages of facts, motivations, incidents, times, places, people. I ring to gain entry. It is a fine summer day in Chichester, a Saturday. My appointment is for nine o'clock and already the city is coming to life. I know that I have a hard day ahead of me and cannot be distracted by other people's lives. My uncle is a policeman and has told me what to expect. The police will be very understanding and will believe me, he says. But I do not believe that; as yet I am not sure I even believe myself.

For years I have waited for this moment, to set out my accusations. It is in black and white in my small plastic bag, ready to have its day in court. There will be no day in court, this I know. Fogarty is dead, and all the deeds of his life, all blame, all responsibility has died with him. I speak in the empty court of posterity. Today I shall state the case for the prosecution.

It is over surprisingly quickly. It takes a little less than an hour, and two cigarettes, and thirty milligrams of diazepam, to get the truth out in the open. Not so very far away the body of Fogarty rests, in the graveyard where we took my father's body to be cremated. I feel them both with me now. Outside, I wait for my mother. Furtively smoking cigarettes while I wait for her distinguished black car. I had sent her away from this shameful place. So much that is so bad is brought to bear on the people who work here: rapes, abductions, murder. Today I have murdered the reputation of my rapist. I do not know then what I know now, that this was the moment of the creation of the English literary canon.

*

Dr Richard Gipps is a doctor twice over, an extravagance of learning. He is a doctor of philosophy and a doctor of psychology. If he has a 'school' I do not know of it. He speaks as he finds, with a gentleness affording a dignity to his patients. I first met Dr Gipps – only when my father died did I dare once to call him Richard – when he was appointed my mentor. Bipolar disorder is a messy general, prepared to sacrifice a lot of men. It was decided that I needed a marshal for my thoughts, that Dr Richard Gipps could be that man. Over the years his good sense has matured into a common ground, a keenness that I make the best of myself and the best of the hand I have been dealt in life. When my father died something changed in our relationship.

A calamity had occurred to Dr Richard Gipps. His child had died, young and suddenly, with his partner, tragically; in the worst possible circumstances. This death brought out the best in Dr Richard Gipps, gave him a wisdom beyond his forty years. Death opened up new avenues for him and for me and gave us a common purpose, a loss, such absence, gave birth to a joint venture, the need to make the most of life.

After all these years, Dr Richard Gipps could see that the truth's destructiveness was a cancer in my being. We tried to discuss my childhood, but I did not have the words to express what had happened to me. A thought was a victory, a sentence almost an impossible thought. I started with the heaviness at my back, and of the boniness 'in' me. Two physical sensations which gather up in their essence what had happened to me, the violation. I thought at first that Fogarty had only been in me physically, but gradually realized that he had been in me mentally and psychically as well. What a rape that was! What perfect thoroughgoing thoroughness. Oh, the achieve of, the mastery of the thing!

I had been mastered by my Latin tutor, taught a new language of debasement and self-annihilation. From 8 September 1987 I had been no longer master of my being, of my soul indeed. What, I began to feel, had allowed this to happen, to happen to me? I did not know. I thought about this a great deal. It was important to me to understand. I thought about cultural relativism, that in another, say, ancient Greek society the love of a boy was not unknown, and did not need to be unknown. But that was the wrong way of thinking, getting things the wrong way about. It was not the physical and psychological act of penetration which afforded me no refuge. It was the shame of it all. In another culture, where shame is not associated with the

act of love between a man and a boy, there is no violation. Unless it be the act of abuse, of forcing himself
on the boy-lover, there is no disgrace. I felt disgrace,
and as a good Catholic, guilt.

I have not yet explained the confessional. For many years
the act of confession took place in a sparsely but politely
furnished study beneath the room in which the sin which
I confessed had taken place. It was many years before I
ventured into the confessional again. I obtained – again
and again, as the hart pants for the stream – absolution
for 'his' crimes, for His crimes, but not release from the
shame and the guilt. Behind the grille of the confessional
I always heard the same words:

'How long has it been since your last confession? Tell me
your sins, that I may absolve you of them in the love of
the risen Christ.'

I have not mentioned yet the music. Oh, the music!
Fogarty instilled in me a deep love of music. Always,
insistently, there was music, seeping into my young,
fertile, febrile mind. Bach, Beethoven, Brahms, Britten
– the wonders of their ages. Fogarty had a vast collection of recordings and one day gave me his vinyls and

a machine to play them on. Unthinkingly, I allowed them into my house, my home, my bedroom. My mother would ask what I was listening to. I did not say the soundtrack of my disgrace, of my despair.

The records have long gone, banished to the attic of my mother's house, to the attic of my mind. My collection of music lies unheard on my shelves in my flat, songs of another time. Will I ever listen to music again – O magnum mysterium – I hope so. But hope is only an audacity of recent times. I am learning not only to speak, but also to hear.

*

I sit down at high table. There is scarcely anyone in tonight. Pip Jasperson at the end of the table. It must be Tuesday. Guest night. No, I remember it's Thursday; hence few guests.

We stand for the dual amphonic grace.

Scholar: *'Benedictus sit Deus in donis suis'*

Response: *'et sanctus in omnibus operibus suis ...'*

I look around the table. There is a neat foreign man opposite.

'... *Deus det vivas gratiam, defunctis requiem: Ecclesiae, Regi-
nae, regnoque nostro, pacem et concordiam: et nobis peccator-
ibus vitam aeternam.*'

'Amen, men.'

The glittering begowned table is seated; opposite me the
stranger. I'll give him a welcome. I know what it is to be
a stranger in this place.

'Good evening.'

He looks up.

'Good evening.'

'I'm Stephen Bernard.'

He takes this in.

'Hello ... Karol Mlynar ... Charles. A friend of Daphne's.'

I don't see her.

'She's running late ... A student.'

Quiet understated conversations start around the table.

'What brings you to Oxford?'

He looks gratified and humoured.

'Oh, you can tell I'm a stranger.'

'The accent. Czech?'

'Yes. I'm here for the Malone conference.'

I don't know him.

'Oh?'

A beat.

'Fascinating man, Malone ...' he says.

The steward brings round the soup.

'Yes.' Pause.

'Fascinating because fascinated. Perhaps?' says the Czech.

I think. Perhaps.

'Indeed,' I murmur.

A pause again. He adjusts his napkin.

'What brought you to Malone?'

I think too for a second.

'Dryden,' I say flatly, although the answer's interesting enough, enough for this.

'Oh?'

'His letters.'

He knows this. I see the knowledge alert in his eyes, reflecting the candle light.

'So many letters ...'

I eat some soup. He continues.

'All found by Malone ... He was keen. He knew where to look. Where no one had.'

Suddenly a door slams and there's a commotion in the far end of the hall. A man, the homeless man from this morning, is there. I recognize him without his great-coat. Even at this distance.

The presiding fellow speaks.

'What's going on?' He looks down the hall. 'Can you see?'

I see it is the homeless man.

'It is a homeless man. I saw him on Broad Street this morning.'

'Really ...'

The presiding fellow lifts his gentle hands from their resting place on the folds of his gown. He thinks for a quick minute. Then turns,

'Oh ... Simon?' He speaks to the attentive, attending steward in his faded white college butler's jacket. The steward steps forward.

'Yes, sir?'

The presiding fellow gestures.

'See that young man down there? See that he is fed.'

Pause.

'Then tell the porters about him. Ask them to phone St Giles. See if they can find him a bed for the night.'

Poor man. Conversation turns back to the supper. The commotion passes. Karol – Charles – is nervously charming throughout dinner but unmemorable; soon I pass into the night.

★

It is a spring day at the clinic. The needle goes in, easily, as it has so often before. You know that the hour is full of promise for you, beckoning. You relax on the bed. A blueish light.

A few moments pass. There is a metallic taste, something with an edge to it. And distinct edges to the things around you, a vibrancy to them. A nurse passes and nods. She seems kind, efficient.

The light changes. You think for a second, catch your thoughts thinking themselves.

Then it comes. It comes now, on a sudden. This is not a thought (you think). It is a revelation. Everything you think. That can be thought. Is intricately connected to everything else. The simple complication of it. This sudden revelation, revealing. This wonder, wondering.

Like a fugue in the mind. The complexity has a clean beauty to it. Tessellations of thought. Thought upon thought. Thoughts reaching out to each other, perfecting each other in a pattern that delineates and completes itself. The mind, this simple thing, perceives it all, encompasses the universe. This. This is it (you think). Now I understand.

You look across at the window, the light playing as it falls across the room. There is a scheme to things, to everything, of which you are part, and now are party. The mind luxuriates in the complexity, this happening.

This thought, which is unique to you. This thought is urgent, needs communicating. You look around, but there is no one to communicate it to, and in fact the words will not come. You want to shout it, but your clamour is stifled in your weakened throat.

You trace your thoughts in the air around you. See them clearly, dancing, but indistinct, losing distinction.

The air from the window opposite is cold. So cold! You feel the chill of ages entering the room, gradually embalming the world in an ice age. Aeons pass. Time is slow (you think).

The nurse looks up at you. You see her, but doubt now her intentions. You see the needle in your hand. You wonder at it, why it is there. That chill! You see the liquid ketamine seeping into your vein. That. That is the cause of this, of these sensations.

You look at your watch. Fifty minutes of the hour have passed. When? You did not notice them. But something has changed, has changed for you in this world. You saw it, had a revelation. All time was there, was here, was now. The rest of your life you will search on the empty steppes of Oxford for it.

You pause in this quickened, quickening room for a moment. You think, are alone with your thoughts. A few minutes pass. You feel tired, like the day has beckoned you but you could not come. Cannot today.

The anaesthetist comes with a bright hello and asks if you are well. You wonder. He takes the needle out. In a minute you will still wonder, at the wonder of it all.

*

I look up. I'm back in the Library. It's deserted after dinner. I must get on with this essay. It's gone eight thirty; the Library closes at ten.

*

From the *TLS* last year:

The title of Cormac Murphy-O'Connor's memoir forms one cardinal's salute to another. In July 1852, John Henry Newman preached at Oscott, near Birmingham, to a gathering of England's recently restored Roman Catholic hierarchy. The country's best-known former Anglican – and its most renowned theologian in 500 years – left some of his hearers in tears by recalling the centuries-long winter through which Catholics had been a despised remnant. Now, he urged, the situation was transformed. His co-religionists were witnessing renewal amounting to 'a second spring'. Though widely deplored in the Church of England as triumphalist, the term was misconstrued by those who missed Newman's careful gloss: 'Have we any right to take it strange, if, in this English land, the spring-time of the Church should turn out to be an English spring, an uncertain, anxious time of hope and fear, of joy and suffering – of bright promise and budding hopes, yet withal, of keen blasts, and cold showers, and sudden storms?

Cold showers, and sudden storms. Murphy-O'Connor in some ways failed the Church, himself, and me in his actions in Sussex in the 1980s and '90s. I lived the consequences of his inaction. Of a Church believing against all odds that it was not the eye of the storm but the 'English spring' in which it was living. This account is my account of what it was like to live in an uncertain, anxious time of hope and fear, of bright promise and budding hopes. This is the grim reality of the English spring, found in the half-lit bedroom of a troubled man in Sussex.

> To some, Murphy-O'Connor's bold title will form an accurate measure of the degree to which his musings disappoint. Apart from the crisis over clerical child abuse, which the Cardinal handles with due contrition insofar as it reflects his poor judgement as a diocesan bishop, the book is more a chronicle of sun, light breeze and scattered showers than of the storms ...

This is the grim reality of the English spring, found in the pages of a literary journal reviewing the apologia of a man who lived in Sussex.

*

Now, I cannot remember how I ended up in all those beds, in all those hospitals, shattered, a broken man. Hopeless, I could not then dream of a world in which I could make a mark, rather I was marked out for nothing by the world, not being for it.

Now, as I lie in my hospital bed, shattered, I cannot remember how I have managed to end up here, in the ketamine clinic at the Warneford, a man with hope, unbroken. I am marked out for something (I think), being now – keenly – for the world.

*

What will survive of me is my books, those I wrote and those I owned. I own a remarkable collection of books, some have said the best personal research library in Oxford. I own hundreds of Lintot's works and all the editions of all the poets whom he published. When I die the collection will be bequeathed to the Bodleian Library, where it will have the shelf mark 'Bernard'.

Fogarty had paper-like, soft, bookish fingers and bony paper-white teeth, but I do not often think of them now when I feel the paper of a book. I feel, when I think of Fogarty, paper cuts. The incision of a caress.

For some years, paper and stickiness and boniness were the only physical sensations I could feel. Now I feel electric – everything, everyone, everywhere – enervated with a glory which defies the past, not just the touch of paper, the sight of white blank pages, and the emissions of the Canon. I ask again, is it possible to love cancer, to be in love with it? The answer must be yes. When you love what rots you, what irradiates you, you gain an enviable power over it and it cannot harm you any longer.

Malone, he after whom the Malone Society is named, was a fine textual editor. He made many startling discoveries in his edition of the letters of Dryden and his work as an editor is a rare example of excellence in the obscure land of scholarship. His letters and books are to be found in the Bodleian Library, where one day my letters will be found, each with their own shelf mark. I have a great affinity for Malone. Lamb knew the pleasures of an Oxford library, the happenstance discoveries of books and men in them, but Malone created part of that library, his life's work – his books and letters – are to be found there, ripe and rich and waiting for discovery. I have edited a lot of letters, and there is an art to having one's letters edited. That art is not to leave behind too much. Of Dryden's letters there are few, of Lintot's there are fewer. By their absences they are recorded in the annals of their times and by that act of recording they shape our perceptions of their times.

Some men burn their letters and by all accounts they are right to do so. By limiting what they leave behind, they delimit the scope for enquiry. Scholarship may seem like an infinite world with infinite possibility, but mankind cannot bear too much reality. The art is in leaving enough behind to leave them wanting more, not everything, as they do not want to know everything, just a few indications that you lived in the world and thought about it.

*

Bernard Lintot, bookseller

Bernard Lintot was, in conscious rivalry with his contemporaries the Tonsons, the preeminent bookseller of the early eighteenth century, towering over the rest. It is not surprising that Tonson has received the most critical attention of any bookseller in the period, but Lintot's promotion of the works of Alexander Pope, starting with the publication of

the twenty-nine-year-old poet's precocious Works
in 1717 was to establish him as a bookseller of con-
siderable importance in the creation of the English
literary canon. His publication of Shakespeare too
was significant, yet these efforts would have been
meaningless, in the long run ...

*

The English literary canon is not all that is best, it is
all that has lasted with the imprimatur of the future
stamped on it. What is the canon? Is it a valid construct? Looking back on my life, for me it is what has
lasted of my intellectual history. Now I write something in the canon, rewrite literary history, have found
the 'lost Augustan': Nicholas Rowe, a writer who owes
his rightful place to me.

Nicholas Rowe was a child of the Williamite dispensation and the first Poet Laureate of the Hanoverians.
His work is almost unknown today, for all his excel-
lencies as a writer. He is the most important writer
in England between the death of John Dryden and
the arrival of Alexander Pope. He bequeaths us some
immortal lines

Guilt is the source of sorrow, 'tis the fiend,
Th'avenging fiend, that follows us behind,
With whips and stings ...

He also gave the world the figure of 'Lothario', the arch seducer. Rowe's reputation was high in his lifetime and for much of the eighteenth century. Only in the last century did his plays fall out of the canon. I have rediscovered him and placed his work again before an appreciative critical audience. What do people remember about Lothario? His seduction of an innocent. What do I remember? As I noticed when I watched *The Fair Penitent* being acted, the body of Lothario lies dead on the stage for all of act five. Lothario is dead for a long time. Fogarty, the seducer of children, was no Lothario, but I will make sure that he is dead for a long time.

*

I only recently began to write this, under the cover of writing, in the Bodleian Library. I do not write of the unchained troubles of the heart. I do not think that I have anything of the eternal in me either, a soul. Nor anything approaching munificent wisdom for all ages either.

A fool – now a professor – once told me that there were only ten things left to be said about English literature, implying that I was not saying any of them. Well, he was not reckoning on this, my discourse on the creation of the English literary canon.

*

I said I would return to Swift. What Swift achieved was mastery of his unbidden, disquieting voice. That to me is a badge of honour. That is the voice of the modern, unencumbered by superstition and ignorance, the daring to speak the silences of eternity. Now I have said the little I have to say about Dryden, Pope, Swift, Hardy and Joyce (nothing), and the others, I can turn briefly to Swift's successor: Evelyn Waugh.

Waugh knew the bitter fruits of comedy and what it was to be an author. He became a Catholic and welcomed into his world the troubles of the cruel world of a comedy found in a handful of dust. He turned the moderns on themselves and found them wanting. What he wanted was to live in a world that lived on the carapace of his creations, the world of P.G. Wodehouse. Wodehouse, and the perfection of him, is found in his unspoken moral universe, of good deeds in a naughty world. There, like Waugh and Orwell, I find a kind of comfort, the generous solicitude of the servant for a child-man; a kind of modern Christ, the ultimate servant giving his life that we might live. Perhaps. While we all admire Bach's Goldberg Variations, what we listen to is often jazz.

*

My work done for the day and curious I look on the internet for relics of the past which has so occupied me today. Oddly perhaps, after all these years, I have never looked up Fogarty on the internet. I am slightly surprised by what I find.

> What it means to be a servant! A reflection on Canon Fogarty R.I.P.
> In the early hours of Monday Morning a great friend of both the diocese and this parish died Canon Fogarty. After over 60 years of dedicated service to the diocese and this local area he will be sadly missed. I have spent some of the week as the news filtered out listening to people remember him and with my reflection on the Gospel this weekend have been able to see why people have remembered him so fondly.

The Gospel readings speak of being a servant to others. To be great in the Kingdom of heaven means to be a servant to others. The word servant has many negative connotations to it. We may think of the servants in the programmes such as Downton Abbey or Upstairs Downstairs but the Christian servant is more than this idea of being a paid servant for a Lord or Lady. To be a servant in the Christian sense is a privilege and also a responsibility it means to be with people through both good and bad times. Jesus wanted to stress that it was not about having power and position 'This is not to happen to you'.

It is being able to be open enough not to be shocked by what you both see and hear. We all have this vocation, as a parent we are servants to our children. It is also very important in the ministry of a priest.

As priests we have the immense privilege of walking with people, sometimes for a short time, through the joys and sorrows of life. I know from what people have told me that the Canon did this countless times. He both buried loved ones but also baptized others and walked with them as they grew up. There was a succession of young people who would seek the canon to go through their work for languages and [he] took a keen interest in their further studies. I am sure [they were] like me seeking that little touch of wisdom we so often get from those who are older than us.

To be a servant then is also about thinking about others and not your own desires, they come second to the needs of others. It is about giving respect and equal dignity to all those whom we come in contact with.

I have learnt, sometimes the hard way, that to be servant for others is both hard and sometimes very frustrating. But, if we live a life of service to others we are living the authentic Christian way. We look to others who have gone before us, recognizing that they too are sinners and in need of God's love and learn from them.

*

Penetration. Of the body, of the mind. An act, and an art. A small masterclass in delicate, but physical, caring, but uncaring, violation. The penis incarnating a theology of abuse in the unwillingly responsive young body. The physical fact annihilates, destroys. The pain, the humiliation. And afterwards, the shame. The blood on the sheets, and later, in my bedroom, on those sheets. Something utterly, exquisitely debilitating. To get from the bedroom to the study is a challenge for the twelve-year-old boy, uncertain of the next move in this break-out role. The locomotion, lavation, ablution, then absolution. A kind of narrative of imperfection leading to perfection. And a pained, sore private part of the body, of the self, telling of the utter violation of the individual, not yet a man. Chosen because he is not yet a man, but chosen because he is not yet a boy either.

*

'This is not to happen to you.'

*

Latin. The language of the Church, the language of canon law. The law does not protect the child, the man protects the child.

*

confessor, *n.*

Etymology: < Latin confessor, and its French repr. confessor, -ur, Anglo-Norman -our (modern French -eur), agent-noun < Latin confitērī to confess v. (In sense 2, Old French had also confes < Latin confessus one who has confessed.) The historical pronunciation, < Anglo-Norman and Middle English confe'ssour, is 'confessor, which is found in all the poets, and is recognized by the dictionaries generally, down to Smart, 1836–49, who has 'confessor in senses 2, 3, con'fesser in sense 1b; for these, Craig 1847 has 'confessor and con'fessor; but con'fessor is now generally said for both.

1. *gen.* One who makes confession or public acknowledgement or avowal of anything.

b. of a crime, sin, or offence charged.

2a. *techn.* One who avows his religion in the face of danger, and adheres to it under persecution and torture, but does not suffer martyrdom; *spec.* one who has been recognized by the church in this character. (The earliest sense in English.)

3. One who hears confessions: a priest who hears confession of sin, prescribes penance, and grants absolution; the private spiritual director of a king or other great personage. Often pronounced /'kɒnfɛsɔː(r)/ in the R.C. Church.

*

What went wrong, what went wrong in Midhurst in the 1980s? What went wrong with me, in the town of Blessed Margaret Pole, witness to the truth of the ages?

> To be a servant then is also about thinking about others and not your own desires, they come second to the needs of others. It is about giving respect . . .

I will show no respect, except to the truth. This is an experiment in autobiography. This may seem an odd comment, so please forgive me, but I am actually finding the piece very interesting as a work of biography. The use of word play, its prose structure, and the examination of language and power are effective in framing such a period in my life.

Biography is such a strange genre. It is often tacitly assumed that the subject retains full agency over the events of their life. What I have presented is a form of biography where the subject loses agency in a most violent way, and yet the act of writing allows him to take some of the power back. I see the piece as partly a comment on biography. One could describe it as postmodern, in that only the biography creates the agency for the subject of the biography.

*

Canon Dermod Fogarty. The servant of the Church. I name you now, now and for ever. You Lothario, you will be dead a long time. I excoriate and curse you. I imprecate you. The English literary canon. I am the creator of the English literary canon. There are two ways of pronouncing the word confessor in English and both mean rape to me: confessor, rape.

*

There is little that is said of Wodehouse. In literary criticism now there is little appreciation of the jouissance, the verve of comedy. There is no forgiveness here in the Faculty for the unforgiving hectic clash of characters in an unreal world. Waugh we can live with, the innocence of Wodehouse is too much to bear. A harsh light spreads itself over the existence of Wodehouse, an existence which I have not yet mentioned, but which in my flat always finds a home.

Dryden, Pope, Swift, and Waugh spoke to the ages, but Wodehouse, if he speaks to any time, speaks to the present in which one reads him, to the moment, outside time. He is the 'new Augustan', the laureate of a better time. The rill of his voice contains a perfection I do not fully understand. His modulations, his idiolect, casts up the promise of an eternal sunshine. I eagerly listen to the syncopations of his time and place, and relish his welcome into a world without responsibility unto anything but the code of one's public school and the moral insistence of a maiden in distress.

I did not think that I would end with an encomium on one of the finest writers of the last century's favourite author, on a moral order which ceased to exist even before Waugh was born, and which even he knew, they both knew, was a confidently uttered untruth. Perhaps we all yearn for the past to come to perfection in the moment, which is what Wodehouse achieves, and what Waugh sees him as achieving. Even when Wodehouse wrote, there were few earls in New York, and fewer aunts worth writing home about. But if writing home about things is half the pleasure, it is most of the accomplishment. This new mode sits easy on my shoulders, but uneasy lies the head that wears the crown of autobiography. Have I said all I have to say? Enough. Does anyone want to hear more? Enough already. Do I regret writing out at last? As that most insightful of writers, Pontius Pilate, said,

'What I have written, I have written.'

*

It is the evening of the May Ball. I have changed into my evening clothes and am feeling the full weight of expectation behind me and my white tie and tails. I have dined out at the Old Parsonage, coming into the college for the dancing. Like every May Ball I have ever been to, I have no partner, which is unusual. These balls are events for brilliant, young, entitled couples, one of which I have never been in. I am the only person not to have a partner this evening, and feel the lack, but also a solitary dignity and a thrill at the promise of it all.

I move under the magnificent gate of the college into the evening. All around me is the loud reassurance of privilege. The men look very fine in their tails (I think). There is something uncomfortable to me about such opulence. I wonder what we have all done to deserve this, what the men and women of Oxford have ever done to deserve this.

The music has already started. In the Main Quad, on the lawns, a small orchestra is perhaps unwittingly playing a song of the last days of the Austro-Hungarian Empire. On no other night would people choose to listen to this. The lights are astonishing. I know everyone as I move through the evening. Everyone is connected to everyone else, and will be for the rest of their lives, having shared this moment of utmost privilege. I catch conversations, rich with delight, as I move, acknowledging others from my singleness.

In the distance, in the corner of Radcliffe Square, there is a ferris wheel slowly picking up the promise of the evening, with a view over the college, the Bodleian Library, and the University Church. I walk back out of the college and towards it. The wheel catches me up in the joy of the moment. I am alone in my box, being lifted up past the quiet confines of the empty library. The chapel to my left tinkles with the sound of champagne glasses.

I am high up now, moving slowly alongside the balcony of the Radcliffe Camera. I think about all the names from the eighteenth century engraved on the glass there, where no one can see them now. Such assumption, passing into posterity. The music is indistinct far below me. The rafts of light, shining up from the quads, are magnificent, filling the evening with intense rightness. This evening belongs to the college.

Now, this moment, at the apex of the turning wheel, I feel a total stillness and a quiet. In my white tie and tails, I expect everything of the world, for it to acknowledge me and my place in it, this evening, alone. I cannot hear the music at all below me now. I know that all is right in the world, for me at least. In this moment of reassurance and expectation I can expect nothing more than this (I think), I feel that I have arrived at an acceptance of things, as the wheel turns, is still for a moment, above the dreams and expectations of a generation.

*

I understand enough Latin, the language of conquest, and Anglo-Saxon, the language of a worried nation which is not yet a nation. My club of failed suicides saves itself for a future which has not yet been constructed. I am no longer the Mendelssohn of suicides. I am a new music which I can slowly but certainly bear to listen to. The truth of my childhood is now the handmaiden of posterity. This. This small world on the edge of the Sussex Downs, where unspeakable things happened, is the beginning of a new nation. The language is English, and in my marketplace is found all literature, at least the literature of England. That is my haven. Oxford is now, as it always was in my mind, my home. Whole vistas of possibility open out to me as I step over the threshold of the Bodleian Library into the chill embrace of the January evening, worlds of meaning as yet unknown to me cry out for discovery.

*

one dark night. one dark. one dark night. fired with love's urgent longings – ah! the sheer grace! – one dark. one dark. dark. dark. night. fired with love's. with love's. urgent. urgent longings.

That music, that noise

– ah! the sheer. sheer grace – dark. dark. urgent. urgent. longings. I went out unseen. my house now being all. being all stilled. in darkness. in darkness, and secure. in darkness and secure. by the secret ladder. disguised. in darkness and concealment.

That music again. Insistent. Urgent.

in darkness, and secure. by the secret ladder, disguised. in darkness and concealment. my house being now all stilled. – ah! the sheer grace! – one dark. one dark night. fired with love's. with love's. with love's urgent. longings. – ah! the sheer grace! – fired with love's. with love's. with love's urgent longings. in darkness. in darkness, and secure by the secret ladder, disguised. in darkness and concealment. love's urgent longings. let us rejoice and be pleased in Him. In darkness and concealment.

amen. men.

This is true.

I gently remove the hand – Fogarty's – from my thigh it comes back it moves towards my groin I do not want this to happen again I can't breathe I'm only little this is wrong I'm scared I can't breathe I'm all by myself with this man he tells me to go upstairs I have no choice I am electric

This is true.

My back is awkward I move and this causes a sudden penetrating force the weight is inside me and intense and above me behind my back green and beige a mirror with an open door in it

I am electric

*

My day's work done, I pass along St Giles, up by the church. I see him, without his greatcoat. The man from this morning. Shivering in the night, begging for some small change. I check my pockets. I have none.

I'm too self-conscious to go to the Old Parsonage for a coffee, my intention. I look down the long wide street of St Giles past the Eagle and Child to the Taylorian. Christminster and its inhabitants. Oxford!

*

Yesterday, I went back to Midhurst. I walked down the lanes and past St Mary's Presbytery in the cool, grey light of the Sussex winter. How small it seemed, and ordinary. Hardly hidden, as you might have expected, behind its low, red brick wall, with its church and the white marble statue of Christ in the gardens.

I was struck by how mundane the details of evil are. That, I suppose, is what is shocking about them. A man, a boy. A house, a bed. How very ordinary, and extraordinary too.

How many winters have passed since yesterday! The truth will tear up those fine lawns, rock that sacristy. The church there will sing the dual antiphony of soiled innocence and long-to-be-regretted indifference. In the pale, weak light of John Henry Newman's 'English spring', it will sound throughout Sussex, which harboured it and hid it, with sadness and sorrow.

I remember the oil painting of St Peter's Basilica on the wall in the presbytery. It is not the presbytery but St Peter's which in my mind is the setting for what happened to me. That has something to match the scale of what happened. I worry that I have made rape seem like an aesthetic experience. That is not my intention. But the tools of aestheticism – the Kantian sublime – are all I have to describe the exquisiteness of the horror and order of what happened.

★

I return through the night to Jericho and my small flat, my home. One, two tablets. Four, nine tablets.

I turn in for the night. It's quiet outside. Inside soon I'm sleeping. I dream as I fall asleep and think as I dream. My day is done now, for the day.

*

I do not believe in ghosts (I think). I am alone in my bedroom in Oxford, at night. I see him there, not quite seen there, reaching over me, his hand holding down my arm and tracing a figure on my skin. It is an old man's hand, but it is ageless to me. I hear him whispering in my ears, but cannot catch what he says, that man. I am tense with expectation and fear. I am not a child reliving the trauma of the distant past, but a forty-year-old man, terrified by a man sometime since dead, in this room, now.

I do not believe in ghosts (I think). I wonder at this, this preoccupation, this occupation of my mind by this man.

*

'Do you think Canon Fogarty is God?' Dr Richard Gipps asked one day.

I thought about this carefully for a moment.

'A god,' I replied.

I thought then of the pantheon of Greek and Roman gods, and of Fogarty being a violent god, the god of violation. There was some comfort to think of this immortal influence on my life being diminished to a godhead. What had this god done to me, done in this mortal world to a child? Why had he done it? It seemed to me that there was something of the eternal in his actions, of an immense and endless evil operating in the world, a boundless malevolence.

And yet he was civilized. He operated also in a world of intricacy and considered thinking. The canon law was his realm, in which he was able to advise and deliver judgements on how people should conduct themselves in this interface between the immortal and the body. Literature, language, music, the civilized arts were his, this minor god of ruination. He instilled in me a love of them, and then a dread of them, of what they meant to me. I worked now in a world where they needed to be explained and understood, but what I needed to explain and understand was Fogarty. I knew how; I wondered why.

'A god', I thought, sadly, terrified at the world in which I live.

★

(I think) I'm more interesting than I'm interested. Reading this, this love letter to my friends, my work, to Oxford, you might wonder that I have any friends at all, or whether Oxford might not be unlovable. You are not the only person to have thought of that – I wonder myself. I am not here to be liked, but to be believed and understood. If I had had a relationship, known what it is to be loved by a man, then ... But I have not, and am the product of three authors: Fogarty, yes, but also Swift and Waugh. I am not a child of Wodehouse, although I revel and divert myself in his childhood world.

As I say, loving cancer means never having to say that you are sorry. But I am sorry, sorry that this happened to me, to anyone. But it did happen. This, my history of the English literary canon is also my perverse love-hate letter to the authors of my being. I would like to end on a note of universal love, of triumphant vindication and exultant all-conquering reconciliation, in English, the all-conquering language of love, but, as I say, in the end all are compromised here at the limits of evil, which I have known in Sussex. Which I know here, now, here in the dark heart of England.

A few words a victory, a sentence an impossible thought? This is my victory, my impossible thought: I would like to end on a note of optimism, in this story about love. The English spring for me has been a time of renewal, though the relationship at the heart of it is cancerous. That is my tale of love. Am I in recovery, remission, I wonder? I would like to hope so, but cancer is a life sentence. It can always come back.

This book has been the work of a few idle hours, sitting in the quiet comfort and dark visibilities of the Bodleian Library. It has been a pleasure to write what I know most about, and although I may not have spoken the truth, I have been truthful.

When I finished the *Curious Incident*, I was exhilarated and saddened: exhilarated because of the deftness of the conclusion, saddened because Christopher had his complex life, with its complications, still to live beyond its pages. We must all do this (I think).

*

It has taken scarcely any time at all to write this, my disquisition on the English literary canon, but in fact it is the result of many years of writing, and not writing. First, there was the sensation: I can't breathe. Why? What was it that was so awful? Then months, years, of careful, considered thinking about this. I can't breathe – so simple and yet so denying of life, of living, the essential requirement for living.

There were the thoughts, straightforward enough: he dropped his pants. He put his penis in. A bare narrative of sorts, with verbs; at least it was being verbalized. Then came the feeling. It hurt. So much hurt, and so few words to put it in. The vocabulary of English is expansive, is expanding, but it seemed, at least at first, not to be enough to encompass what had happened. It hurt.

So, Dr Richard Gipps and I started. First with the sensations, of stickiness, of the in-ness of the action, the act of someone being in one. That was the violation, of body, of mind. But the mind came first, first of all. The violation was mental, and then we found it was also intellectual, theological, and in fact, historical. But that last fact is only now, now as I record the actions of what happened in Sussex in the 1980s, becoming true. This is an historical document, speaking out, writing out what happened under the watchful, not watchful eye of the bishop of Arundel and Brighton.

It was complicated. At least at first. It is complicated even now, now after all these years of discussion, of thinking, and of more discussion. Something cosmic, of the order of creation, had happened to me. That it is hard to comprehend. That there was created in that moment, those moments, a theology of violation, of the child wronged. Something spectacular in its scope was begun, a series of thoughts set in motion in the bedroom, in the study, in the confessional. At the heart of it was the creator, in that moment of creation, the divine being was made complicit in the actions of a disturbed but orderly man in Sussex, a man cloaked in the blackness of his church. He was not at the English College in Rome then, but was he very far from it? It too was made part of what happened, made part of the weft of my life. That institution, which I have never seen, will never see, was made complicit too in these creative destructive acts.

So, Dr Richard Gipps and I continued, carefully reconstructing the self from the waste years. These were not the 'wilderness years', they were about wasted years, of missed opportunities, chances to be reborn. The word was made flesh and the word was man. Flesh, that simple encarcasement, something instinctive, feeling, with thoughts and emotions, unthinking, unfeeling, was made urgently present to me.

The presence of the other. The other man, but not the other man I wanted or welcomed, although I accepted that in that strong, intellectual, theological thinking being was something of the order of creation. Was this what it was all about? This abuse, this violation? Was that the reason for existing in the world, to be made flesh, to be made man. Was this what it meant to be a man?

I can't breathe

That, that denial of the very force for life was the only absolution I ever received in that study in Sussex. It hurt. It hurts still. It hurt then and it will always hurt, this, that.

*

I sit at my desk, think, and write a letter to myself from myself for the morning and place it in my pocket.

All the urgency is gone now. I have done it. I have created an historical document, which puts the record straight about what happened in Sussex in the 1980s. I can set it to one side for the moment, having done it. Now I can get on with living my life, with the work I have to do, with Dr Gipps; academically. It is wonderful to think that I have created something so clear and honest about what happened. But that is not my life, which is to be lived now. I have had the sense that I spin a lot of discs in my life of which this was just one. Now, for the moment, that disc can continue to spin of its own accord. I am glad that I wrote it, that it is written. All the urgency of it, of this day, has gone, now that it is done, for now. It has been a protracted labour and the child is not what I expected, but is wonderful. It is me.

Today was the day it all came right. Unbidden, as I sleep I deconstruct the self.

Sleep now, sleep. Rest, rest.

Canon Fogarty's headstone and memorial were destroyed by the Roman Catholic Church on 24 May 2018, three months after the first publication of this book in hardback.

ACKNOWLEDGEMENTS

With thanks to my family and friends Michael Caines, Richard Clay, Hugo Evans, Joanna Gray, Phoebe Griffith, John McTague, Verity Platt, and Claudine van Hensbergen. For encouraging me as a mentor and doctor, I should like to thank Dr Richard Gipps. For seeing some potential in this book, I should like to thank my brilliant literary agent, Caroline Dawnay, and Sophie Scard. For their diligent and fine editing of this book, I should like to thank Dan Franklin and Bea Hemming. For the preparation of the manuscript, I should like to thank Ana Fletcher and Alex Russell. For her elegant artistic work, I should like to thank Suzanne Dean. For help with the Czech, my gratitude is due to Standa Zivny. For help with the French, my gratitude is due to Michèle Mendelssohn. I should like especially to thank Felicity James for her constant encouragement.

The author and publishers gratefully acknowledge permission to reprint material from the following copyright holders. While every effort has been made to acknowledge copyright holders, if any have inadvertently been overlooked the publishers would be happy to correct this in future editions.

Caitlin Moran, 'He wired us to ourselves', *The Times*, 2016. © Caitlin Moran. Reproduced by permission of the author c/o Rogers, Coleridge & White Ltd., 20 Powis Mews, London W11 1JN

T.S. Eliot, 'East Coker', *The Poems of T.S. Eliot*, two vols., ed. Christopher Ricks and Jim McCue (London: Faber and Faber, 2015), 1.193 © The Estate of T.S. Eliot

Dennis Duncan, 'Hoggs that Sh–te Soap, p. 66', *Times Literary Supplement*, 15 January 2016, 14–15 © Dennis Duncan

Rupert Shortt, 'Encoded', *Times Literary Supplement*, 15 July 2015, 8–9 © Rupert Shortt

Peter Fitch, 'What it means to be a servant' [http://peterfitch31.blogspot.co.uk/2012/10/what-it-means-to-be-servant-reflection.html accessed 14 January 2016] © Peter Fitch

INDEX

Ackermann, Rudolph, 128
Addison, Joseph, 15, 68
  The Campaign, 68
  The Spectator, 14–15
Africa, dark heart of, 31; *see also* Haggard, H. Rider
American Hospital, Paris, 96–97
Anglican Church, 14, 39, 61, 67
Anglo-Saxon, 175
Anne, Queen, 64
Ap Gryffyd, Matthew, 132–33
Arundel and Brighton, bishop of, *see* Murphy-O'Connor, Cardinal Cormac

Bach, Johann Sebastian, 147
  Goldberg Variations, 165
Bacon, Sir Francis, 86
Bayley, John, 130
BBC News 24, 129
Beaumont Street, Oxford, 11
Beckett, Samuel, 105
Bede, 62
Beethoven, Ludwig van, 147
Beerblock, 100

Bentley, Richard, 64–65
Berkeley, George, 86
Bernard, Gerard, 5, 16, 18, 23, 34, 37, 60, 70, 77, 83, 94, 103, 136–137, 145
  death, 103, 127, 144,
Bernard, Helen, 23, 29, 40, 77, 103, 104, 143,
  caring nature, 104
Bernard, Margaret, 5, 16, 17–18, 23, 34, 60, 77, 103–04, 121, 127, 135, 136–137, 142, 143, 144, 146
  absolution, 104
  strength, 103
Bernard, Stephen, 9–10, 15, 48, 69, 77, 149
  and bipolar I disorder, *passim*
  and confession, 20, 28, 34, 73–74, 147, 185
  and ketamine, 7, 112, 115, 116–119
  and Roubiliac's bust of Pope, 74
  and Sherborne School, 14, 38, 39, 43, 51, 53–54, 55, 60, 61, 67, 80
  and the multiverse, 7, 106
  appearance at twelve, ix

Bernard, Stephen (*continued*)
  constructs the self, 3–6, 9, 48
  email to Dr Richard Gipps, xi
  estrangement from the Roman
      Catholic Church, 38, 40, 137
  flat in Oxford, 3–7, 24, 127,
      128–129, 180
  Junior Research Fellowship, 40
  library of, 159
  on biography, 43, 170–71
  on children, 104, 108–109
  on Latin, 17, 18–19
  scholarship to Sherborne School,
      Dorset, 14
  statement to the police, 32–41
  suicide attempts, 54–58, 96–97,
      109
  wit, 44, 47–48
  see also Sherborne School, Dorset;
      Oxford, University of
Betterton, Thomas, 8, 124
Bible, The, 20
Boone, Christopher, 113
Bowie, David, 4–5
Boyle, Charles, 64
Brahms, Johannes, 147
British Empire, 21, 31
Britten, Benjamin, baron, 147
Broad Street, Oxford, 12, 97, 131, 152

Caedmon, 62
Cambridge, University of, 100
canon law, 16, 18–19, 168, 181
Catullus, 12, 19
Central Military Hospital, Prague,
    109
Chance, David, 39, 69–70, 78
Charles I, King, 131
Chichester, West Sussex, 127, 143
Christminster, 12, 87–93, 88
Coetzee, J.M., 25, 49
  Disgrace, 25
Colvin, Sir Howard, 131

Daily Telegraph, The, 36, 73
Da Vinci, Leonardo, 139
  Vitruvian Man, 139
D'Israeli, Isaac, 65
Dobson, Zuleika, 86
Downton Abbey, 166
Dryden, John, 26–27, 101, 111, 128,
    151–152, 160–161, 162, 164, 171
  sons of, 27
Duncan-Jones, Katherine, 130

Eagle and Child, Oxford, 178
East, Henry, 43, 77, 79–81, 83
Ede & Ravenscroft, Oxford, 83
Edinburgh, University of, 80
Eisner, Didi, 9, 53–54, 77, 98,
    104–105, 107, 114, 138
  excellence of, 105
Eisner, Hans, 53
Elgar, Sir Edward:
  The Dream of Gerontius, 55
Eliot, T.S., 61, 67
English College in Rome, 16, 73, 185
Elizabeth II, Queen, 84
Essen, Odette van, 77, 110

Ferrar, Nicholas, 67
Fielding, Henry:
  Tom Jones, 8
Finch, countess of Winchelsea, Anne,
    134
Findlay, Mrs, 72
Fogarty, Canon Thomas 'Dermod',
    vii, 3, 16–17, 18–19, 20, 22, 25,
    31–41, 43, 44–47, 49–50, 61,
    67–68, 69, 71–74, 77, 78, 104,
    116, 118, 136–37, 138, 144,
    146, 147, 159–160, 163, 165,
    171, 177, 180–182
  and abuse of the confessional, 20,
    28–29, 34, 41–42, 73–74, 147,
    171, 185
  and Bernard, *passim*

and the English College in Rome, 16, 73, 185
appearance, 16
death, 137–138
obituary, 165–167
Font-Romeu-Odeillo, France, 75
Fortescue, John, 114, 115, 118, 119

Gipps, Richard, viii, 78, 144ff
email from Stephen Bernard, xi
Gjielo, Ola:
Dark Night of the Soul, 10, 132, 176
O Magnum Mysterium, 10, 21, 74, 132, 148
God, *passim*
Godchester, Bill, 79, 83
Godolphin, Sidney Godolphin, first earl of, 8, 9
Greek, 49
Green's, Mayfair, 95
Grenadier, Knightsbridge, 95

Haddon, Mark, 25, 113–114, 127
The Curious Incident of the Dog in the Night-time, 25, 114, 183
Haggard, H. Rider:
She, 31
Hedge, Jerry, 59
Heyshot, Alice, 86
Hollinghurst, Alan:
The Swimming-Pool Library, 37
Hommes International, 34
Holmes, Sherlock, 114
Hume, David, 86

Ingamells, Andrew, 100, 128
Italy, 54

Jackson, John, 99–100
Jasperson, Pip, 148
Jerome, Sister, 34
John, Mother, 38
Johnson, James, 77, 106–107, 129

Johnson, John, 99
Johnson, Samuel, 64 [*sic*]
Josephus, 111
Joyce, James, 25, 164
Finnegans Wake, 25

ketamine, 7, 112, 114–120, 154–156; *see also* Bernard, Stephen
Fortescue, John
King Edward VII Hospital, Midhurst, 23
King, William, 64–65

Lamb, Charles, 138, 160
Lamb, Mary, 138
Latin, 17, 18, 19, 32, 44–47, 49, 125, 146, 168, 169, 175
Lawrence, T.E., 52
L'Estrange, Sir Roger, 111
Lintot, Bernard, 13, 66, 77, 101–102, 106, 110–111, 112, 132, 159, 161–162
Little Gidding, Cambridgeshire, 67
Liverpool, 14, 134
London, 63, 80, 134
London Bridge Street, 133
London Gazette, The, 124

Malone, Edmund, 13, 133, 150–152
Malone Society, The, 160
Malory, Sir Thomas, 98
Marlborough, John Churchill, first duke of, 8–9, 68, 125
Martial, 17, 19
Martyrs' Memorial, Oxford, 10, 130
McFergus, Fergus, 77, 110
Mendelssohn, Felix, 55–56, 175
Michelangelo, 85
Midhurst Grammar School, Midhurst, 23
Midhurst, West Sussex, 28–29, 32–41, 44, 51, 62, 127, 170, 178–179
Mlynar, Karol, 149–153

Moya, Hidalgo, 100
Mulgrave, Sunny, 77, 108–109; *see also* Normanby, Richard; Normanby, Hattie
Murdoch, Iris, 130
Murphy–O'Connor, Cardinal Cormac (formerly bishop of Arundel and Brighton), 36, 135–158, 185
  failings of, 36, 158, 185

Negus, Richard Frederic, 51–53, 54
Newman, Cardinal John Henry, 19, 157
  and the 'English spring', 157–158, 179
Norfolk, dukes of, 28–29
Normanby, Hattie, 63, 108
Normanby, Richard, 77, 108–109; *see also* Mulgrave, Sunny; Normanby, Hattie
Nowell, Alexander, 99

Oates, Titus, 26
Old Parsonage Hotel, Oxford, 173, 178
Orwell, George, 165
Oscott, Birmingham, 157
Ovid, 49
Oxford, 24, 59, 63, 102, 118, 124, 127, 128, 129, 130, 133, 156,
Oxford, University of, 10, 14, 41, 42, 48, 50, 53–54, 68, 78, 79, 83–84, 94, 98, 99, 100, 110, 150, 160, 173, 176, 178, 182
  Balliol College, 130
  Blackwell Hall, Bodleian Library, 50, 76
  Bodleian Library, 10, 12–13, 42, 50, 76, 97, 111–112, 121, 124, 129, 132, 133–134, 139, 141, 142, 156, 159, 160, 163, 174, 176, 183,

Brasenose College, 98–100, 101
  quincentenary, 100
Christ Church, 51–52, 54, 85, 87, 93, 94, 108, 138
Clarendon Building, 97
Hertford College, 141
St John's College, 53, 130–131
The Queen's College, 79
The Taylorian Institute, 178
University College, 40, 100–101, 118
Worcester College, 11–12

Paris, 51, 59, 96–97, 134
Pemberton, R.A., 77, 81–82
Pevsner, Nicolas, 29
Pilsdon Manor, Dorset, 39, 60–61, 67
Pole, Blessed Margaret, 28, 170
Pontius Pilate, 173
Pope, Alexander, 26–27, 74–75, 101–102, 128, 161, 162, 164, 171
  Dunciads, 8
  The Works of Alexander Pope, 112, 142, 162
Powell, Philip, 100
Prague, 51, 59, 131, 134
Praxiteles, 16
Prior, Peter, 51–52, 57–58, 59, 81

Repton, Anne, 77, 135, 138–139
Rex, Darius, 80
Richardson, Samuel, 25, 49
  Clarissa, 25, 49
Roman Empire, 20
Roman Catholic Church, 17, 18–19, 20, 23, 24, 26, 27, 28, 29, 38, 45, 47, 67, 70, 74, 135, 136, 137, 158, 168, 169, 171, 178–179
Royal Military Academy, Sandhurst, 82
Roubiliac, Louis Francois:
  Alexander Pope, 74

Rowe, Nicholas, 49, 111, 124, 162
   The Fair Penitent, 163
   *The Plays and Poems of Nicholas
      Rowe*, 49
Rugby, Michael, 37
Ruskin, John, 53

Samson, William, 36
Scott, Tom, 94–96
Selden's Map of China, 76
Shakespeare, William, 49, 130, 162
   The Rape of Lucretia, 49
Sherborne School, Dorset, 14, 38, 39,
      43, 51, 53–54, 55–57, 60, 61,
      67, 80
Sidney, Sir Philip, 95
Simon (SCR steward), 153
Spenser, Edmund, 95
St Aubyn, Edward, 25, 49
   Some Hope, 25
St Giles, Oxford, 9, 10, 12, 153, 178,
St Margaret's Convent School, Mid-
      hurst, 29, 35, 38
St Mary's Presbytery, Midhurst,
      23, 29, 33, 34, 35, 37, 39, 43,
      44–47, 62–63, 178–179
St Peter's Basilica, Rome, 45, 179
Steele, Daphne, 100, 149
Stoppard, Tom:
   The Invention of Love, 81
Stoughton, Kathleen, 61
Swift, Jonathan, 26–27, 164, 171, 182

Tagus, Frederick Wyndham, mar-
      quess of (also known as the
      earl of Sanford), 77, 84–87

Tatler, The, 86
Tennyson, Eleanora, 104–106
Thatcher, Margaret, baroness,
      116–117
Times, The, 4, 82, 117
Times Literary Supplement, The, 13, 23,
      64, 97, 126, 135, 156
Timmins, Charles, 40, 78–79, 98,
      102–103, 115
Tonson the elder, Jacob, 13, 24, 68,
      111, 161
Tonson the younger, Jacob, 13, 111,
      161

University Church of St Mary the
      Virgin, Oxford, 174
Upstairs Downstairs, 166

Van Dyck, Sir Anthony, 85
Vickers, Sir Brian, 130
Victoria, Queen, Empress of India,
      84
Villefranche de Conflent, France,
      75

Walcott, Sir Derek, 98
Walton Street, Oxford, 10, 11
Warneford Hospital, Oxford, 117
Waugh, Evelyn, 164–165, 171–172,
      182
Wilson, A.N., 130
Wodehouse, P.G., 164–165, 171–172,
      182
Wren, Sir Christopher, 100

Yeovil District Hospital, 57–60

If you are a child being sexually abused or have been sexually abused, or have mental health difficulties, or if you are in distress because of either, the following organizations can help:

Childline
0800 111 111
www.childline.org.uk

Police
Free non-emergency telephone number: 101

Mind
0300 123 3393
www.mind.org.uk

Samaritans
116 123
www.samaritans.org